FITCH PATH

A Cautionary Tale About
A Moose, Millennials,
Leadership & Transparency

Todd Corley

ISBN: 1514755769
ISBN 13: 9781514755761

WHAT PEOPLE ARE SAYING ABOUT
FITCH PATH

"I meet with C-suite executives across a wide range of industries, on a regular basis. They see a seismic shift in how today's multicultural generation approaches the implicit and explicit contract between employer and employee. In his debut book, *FITCH PATH*, Todd Corley, a distinguished INROADS alumnus and former Global CDO at Abercrombie & Fitch, provides a blueprint organizations can use to reconcile changing employee expectations with current organizational operations. He offers battle-tested solutions rooted in real-world experience."
--Forest Harper, President & CEO, INROADS, Inc.

"Todd may have had the most challenging corporate Chief Diversity Officer role in the world, over the last decade. Despite that, his character and managerial courage helped him find solutions for the things many organizations face each day: internal headwinds, external accountability, internal engagement and external criticism. *FITCH PATH* offers sound advice on how to prepare for the inevitable new workforce."
--Neil Horikoshi, President & Executive Director, Asian & Pacific Islander Scholarship Fund

"If you know Todd Corley, you know that he understands the Millennial mind and is always ready to teach. He is insightful, provocative, and not afraid to challenge your assumptions. I am excited about *FITCH PATH*, as it is leading edge thinking for how to understand, engage, and motivate the next generation of leaders."
--Darlene Slaughter, Chief Diversity Officer, United Way Worldwide

"In a world of noise and a potential overload of information, Todd Corley brings us clear and useful information in *FITCH PATH*. Through research, his extensive outreach efforts and real world experience, we are given insight into an important part of our diverse world - the world of generational diversity. Millennials/Gen Y employees and citizens have a lot to offer to us, and Todd helps us understand how we can understand and engage this important generation."
--Tanya M. Odom, Global Diversity & Inclusion and Education Consultant, Executive Coach

"Sometimes our most interesting jobs are also our most challenging. Todd's ability to navigate the choppy waters of Abercrombie & Fitch during an EEOC mandated consent decree as Chief Diversity Officer should be a story of failure and frustration. But it's not. Todd's business acumen, diversity chops, and ego-less approach guides this story into triumphant waters because he has mined from that experience a new perspective on the future of our workplace--particularly that this near future multi-generational workplace is where diversity issues will truly bloom. *FITCH PATH* outlines a foresight anyone who cares about the future of work should care about."
--John J. Schaffner-former Sr. Director Talent and Leadership Development, A&F; current Executive Coach and L&D specialist

"Todd Corley is easily one of the foremost authorities on Millennials and iGens in the workforce. His thoughtful, informed, and transparent worldview about change management was honed while navigating difficult cultural and generational challenges at work. The perspectives he offers in *FITCH PATH* can help us better understand and appreciate differences, while also serving as a guide to help spur greater collaboration and productivity among team members of all generations."
--Debra Nelson, Diversity & Inclusion Practitioner, and Head, Corporate Communications, Brasfield & Gorrie

"One of the greatest fears of this generation is to lead a boring life that's not connected to anything meaningful. *FITCH PATH* outlines bold not borrowed best practices for engaging employees, regardless of how new or advanced your D&I initiative is."
--Toya L. Spencer, Vice President, Diversity & Inclusion – Huntington Bank

"*FITCH PATH* outlines the confluence of historical events and social platforms (Facebook, LinkedIn, Twitter) that freed Millennials to choose personal identities from a set of possibilities unprecedented in diversity and individuality. By referencing his time and global perspective at Abercrombie & Fitch, Todd helps all of us to fully appreciate the sense of urgency in creating inclusive workplace policies."
--Fields Jackson, Jr, Founder & CEO, Racing Toward Diversity magazine

(English)
The world continues to shrink and diversity becomes even more important in today's business world. Todd Corley and his book on the ever changing face of diversity is perfectly positioned to paint the needs of the next generation – particularly growing GEN Y and junior managers for the future. Todd's expertise is unparalleled.
--Nathan Y. Andres, PHR – Japan and Southeast Asia Human Resources Professional

(Japanese)
世界の距離が縮まり、現代のビジネス界では多様性が一層重要になっています。絶え間なく変化する多様性についてのトッド・コーリーの著書は、特にジェネレーションY世代（1978年から1990年代半ばに誕生の、ベビー・ブーマーの子どもに当たる世代）や若手マネージャーのニーズを表現するものとして完璧です。トッドは類稀な専門知識を持っています。
ネイザン Y. アンドレス
日本及び東南アジア人事専門

"Despite the distractions that often worked against Todd's D&I strategy, he persuaded a generation of young people (Millennials and iGens) that inclusion trumped exclusion. He reminded them that their call for transparency and authenticity among leaders would be a great benefit to business practices and government policies. *FITCH PATH*, teaches all of us how we got here and where we're headed."
--Reta Jo Lewis, Esq. is a Senior Resident Fellow at the German Marshall Fund of the United States; First-ever Special Representative for Global Intergovernmental Affairs, at the U.S. Department of State, under Secretaries Hillary Clinton and John Kerry in the Obama Administration; and former-Vice President and Counselor to the President at the U.S. Chamber of Commerce.

"Todd's leadership with and use of connective technologies enabled him to build a grassroots campaign that emphasized curiosity and empathy and withstood organizational challenges to make change stick. *FITCH PATH* guides us along a rocky road that shows how bright the future can be if we allow Millennials and iGens to lead the way."
--Sheila Robinson, Publisher & CEO, Diversity Woman Magazine

"Finally a book that moves beyond pat generalizations and stereotypes in describing the newest generations entering the workforce and shaping our global markets. With insights based on direct experience and informed by his ability to mine, shape and leverage social media, Todd Corley helps us see what is both around the corner and on the horizons as young adults move from the classroom to the boardroom. Having witnessed their parents' 24/7 yoke to an insatiable corporate plow that insisted that they continuously do more with less, these emerging leaders are not surprisingly forging a different path."
--Deborah Dagit, Former Vice President and Chief Diversity Officer, Merck; President, Deb Dagit Diversity LLC

"Perhaps you've noticed that a shift has occurred. The success of any organization begins with the engagement of its people. What motivates the workforce of the past is very different from that which motivates the workforce of today. Enter Millennials - sharp, collaborative and hungry to create real change. If you are still wondering about how to do that, you must read Todd's book *FITCH PATH*. Engaging, based upon experience and packed with information that will equip you to lead this next generation."
--Skot Welch, Founder/Managing Partner - Global Bridgebuilders;
Author: 101 Ways to Enjoy The Mosaic

"Todd recognized early that to be successful in his environment he had to be strategic with every decision and intentional with every interaction. Most importantly, he understood the complexities of navigating an unstable organizational culture, while authentically engaging a workforce divided by images and messages of success and identity. Sometimes the conflict between 'doing what's right' and 'managing what's difficult' cannot be reconciled by instinct or deter-mination alone. Todd made a critical decision - engage the workforce population through their generational lens and embed a sense of community that drives sustainable behavioral change. He took a stand and made a difference. *FITCH PATH* offers timely, relevant, solution based lessons that are equally as enlightening as they are inspiring."
--Reginald Butler, CEO, Performance Paradigm, LLC; Executive Coach and D&I Specialist

"Todd's contribution to the D&I space is well known, as the former Senior Vice President & Global Chief Diversity at A&F. His proven ability to work across five different generational groups in that role and create measurable change, is reason enough to read *FITCH PATH*, his debut book. It provides the reader a road map to move the needle in their organization and engage their workforce."
--Steve Francis, President, Central Ohio Diversity Consortium & Manager, Community Affairs, Honda of America

CONTENTS

PREFACE

Millennials first filled my world in November 2004, when I accepted the job of Chief Diversity Officer at Abercrombie & Fitch—a position mandated by the settlement of discrimination lawsuits against the company, totaling nearly $50 million. Millennials, by then, were not only the retailer's workforce but also its market.

As a member of Generation X, I was fascinated by the drastic shifts in culture between my own peers and this younger group. I quickly came to admire their openness, their generosity, their friendships, their priorities, and their effortless command of accelerating technologies. I heard my peers and older people disparage their supposed laziness, self-absorption, and lack of work ethic, but these were not the young people I had come to know.

I wanted to learn more, to understand as fully as I could about this intriguing generation that is our future. I recruited writer Gene Stowe, a Baby Boomer journalist who has observed Millennials since the first ones were born, and researcher Zach Welty, a Millennial with a degree in athropology and inside experience, to help me investigate.

What they reported about the convergence of history and technology in the Millennials' environment enabled me to better understand these amazing men and women. It also gave me greater clarity about who they are. As the first Millennials were aging into the Abercrombie & Fitch workforce, they signaled that they would not tolerate policies and practices that had gone unnoticed or unquestioned by the previous generations. Today, new waves of Millennials continue to do the same, as was evident by a recent Supreme Court decision, 8–1 in favor of a young lady who wore a hijab to a job interview.

Years earlier, *Gonzalez v. Abercrombie & Fitch* was an opportunity, an early warning to transform "business as usual" into the radically more diverse, just, respectful, and open environment of the rising generation. It was a call for Abercrombie & Fitch and *every* other American company to look like America, the real multicultural America that is coming and has already broken out among the young.

For me, the job as diversity officer was an amazing opportunity to engage these remarkable people, to learn from them, to support them, and to help them create better environments, whether that was at work, in their neighborhoods, or within their social circles. It was a unique opportunity to show impressionable young people that the little-traveled road to corporate diversity is filled with real-life teachable moments that you can't make up in a textbook. Since then, I have started my own think tank and advisory group to engage Millennials and iGens—and the older generations who hire, manage, teach, sell to, and otherwise relate with them.

Many in the older generations remain pessimistic about the future. They see Millennials and iGens rejecting the rigid, static, hier-archical approach that kept the old system running, and they fear a collapse. My experience with these people suggests the opposite: the more their collegial, collaborative, results-oriented approach ascends, the better for business and for society. They make me look forward to the future with great hope.

Todd Corley

FITCH PATH

A Cautionary Tale About A Moose,
Millennials, Leadership & Transparency

Todd Corley

INTRODUCTION

As the Millennial workforce swells and iGens (Gen Z) increasingly join them, the demand for trusted, transparent, and authentic leadership is reaching unprecedented heights. By leveraging social media and manifesting a remarkable openness and quest for inclusion, these younger generations are forging cultural shifts that upend traditional leadership values and practices. Traditionalists and Baby Boomers, who resist the call for more equitable and ethical workplaces and seek to maintain "business as usual" leadership, place themselves and their organizations at grave risk, regardless of industry or sector. By 2020, Millennials and iGens will compose nearly 60 percent of the U.S. workforce. Preparing your leadership and organization for that eventual reality is mission critical: transparency has become the new normal.

Perhaps shaped by the ease of their communication with a vast range of diverse colleagues, acquaintances, and friends, the natural tendency of these generations is to focus on purpose and people rather than profit alone. It's undeniable that this trend toward wanting more familiarity, comfort, and trust among one another is here to stay. The evidence is everywhere you turn – across major cities, rural communities, or small hamlets. Simply look at the rise of the "sharing economy," where we see strangers willing to hop into a stranger's car (Uber) or spend the night in an apartment of someone you have never met while visiting a country that you have always wanted to visit (Airbnb). This is more than an economic breakthrough; it's a cultural one, and a tipping point.

FITCH PATH aims to elevate the understanding of these generations and their promising, transformative role in the story of corporations, institutions, individuals, and society. I saw the impact of Millennials and the rising iGens during my years at Abercrombie

& Fitch's home office on Fitch Path in New Albany, Ohio. First-wave Millennials, acting on their instinct for equality, brought about dramatic change in the company that has been an American institution since the nineteenth century. The resulting Abercrombie & Fitch path to a twenty-first-century workforce is both a cautionary tale and a model to celebrate.

This book tells that story, focusing on the historical, wide-reaching social issues and technological advances that shaped the Millennials who acted with courage, respect, and passion to challenge the status quo in *Gonzalez v. Abercrombie & Fitch*. They achieved a radical workforce transformation by remaining purposeful and authentic while I, a Gen Xer, learned to build familiarity, comfort, and trust through an innovative and sometimes disruptive inclusion strategy that engaged them on their maturing personal journeys or redirected them at times when they were filtering competing messages of inclusion versus exclusion.

It's a firsthand account of how hundreds of thousands of young people for ten years committed themselves to making a difference, becoming self-aware instead of self-absorbed. It's the story of my ongoing efforts to implement an inclusive vision as the Millennials are all grown up and their successors, the iGens, come of age. This story aims to elevate understanding among generations and to propose an approach that can uplift everyone.

Chapter 1

THE CHALLENGE:
RACING TOWARD DIVERSITY

In June 2003, Eduardo Gonzalez was waiting with the others for the start of the press conference in San Francisco to announce a class-action discrimination lawsuit against Abercrombie & Fitch by nine former or would-be employees representing an untold number of workers. One of the lawyers casually mentioned that his name would be on the lawsuit—*Gonzalez v. Abercrombie & Fitch*. That was news to him. Gonzalez had figured it might be his friend Anthony Ocampo, who had worked a Christmas rush for A&F in Glendale before he was turned down at the San Mateo store near Stanford University where they went to school. Or maybe one of the Asian Americans who had once worked for the Crystal Court Mall store for more than two years, like Jennifer Lu. The list of names ran deep, originating with Juancarlos Gomez-Montejano's EEOC complaint in 1999, and including a young woman named Brandy Hawk from New Jersey.

His name out front? Whatever it took. This wasn't personal to him, like one of the other guys who had wept at losing his dream job. And he was jaded enough to assume nothing would come of it, a bunch of young people against a giant corporation. But Gonzalez figured something had to be tried. More than 90 percent of the company's twenty-two thousand employees were white, a seemingly disproportionate amount for a company that was trying to sell to people of his generation. He remembered the day of the group interview—he was in dress slacks and shirt, everyone else in t-shirts and flip-flops. After the group interview, he went across the hall and instantly landed a job at

Banana Republic.

When Ocampo told him about the emerging lawsuit, Gonzalez signed up. On April 25, 2003, Gonzalez filed a charge of discrimination with the Equal Employment Opportunity Commission (EEOC), and a few days later, he received a copy of his Notice of Right to Sue from the California Department of Fair Employment and Housing (DFEH). The named plaintiffs got training on how to speak to the press. Eventually, a *New York Times* reporter and photographer came to his house for a story. From this point on, every reference to the case would bear his name: *Gonzalez v. Abercrombie & Fitch.*

Who were these upstart litigants who reshaped the self-conscious symbol of American youth and coolness? They were the leading edge of a new generation, named Millennials because they came of age at the start of the third millennium, three generations removed from Abercrombie's leadership. Heirs to the Civil Rights Movement, brought up amid accelerating communication and connection technology, Millennials demanded a different world, a world of inclusion, equality, openness, and respect regardless of difference. They were determined to change not only the structures and processes of corporations and communities but also the psychology and values—insisting on personal attributes of openness and inclusion often in direct contrast to the rules and taboos of the past.

In the following chapters, we will examine the factors that have shaped Millennials, especially in the United States but also around the increasingly interconnected world, and the evidence that they are already having a powerful impact on that world.

Chapter 2

THE MILLENNIALS

I f you are a Millennial, this is for you. If you love, manage, supervise, live with, sell to, buy from, or know a Millennial, this is for you, too. It is not an attempt to define or explain Millennials, to propose or support a thesis about Millennials. It is, rather, an attempt to acknowledge that Millennials ought not to be classified, pigeonholed, or evaluated—whether in praise or blame—as an identifiable monolithic category. It is an attempt to recount the confluence of historical and technological forces that freed Millennials to choose personal identities from a set of possibilities unprecedented in diversity and individuality. It aims to describe the environment where this generation has grown up—the soil, the water, the air, the climate—in full awareness of the rich variety that has flowered and flourished in that environment. It aims to reflect the same respect for individuality that Millennials overwhelmingly display to each other, to their elders, and to those who follow them.

Millennials, the generation previously known as Generation Y because they followed Generation X, might well be called "Generation Why Not?" The question can be the impatient appeal of a teenager to a parental refusal, and it can be the ringing call to progress: "Some men see things as they are and ask why. I dream things that never were and ask why not." Such is the diversity of a generation for whom progress is a constant and change is a given. The fact that a person was born after 1981 is no predictor of how they will ask the question, much less how they will answer it. Some Millennials are at least as likely to disagree with other Millennials as well as with their elders—they neither expect nor offer generational solidarity, and they do not appreciate generational stereotyping. The reasons for this diversity, as we will see, have to do with their context in history and their unprecedented access to technology.

The naming of generations to organize history, rather than, say, rulers (twentieth dynasty, Victorian era, Ming dynasty), is a recent and initially American phenomenon. The fact of the population explosion produced by returning World War II soldiers—nearly eighty million people—naturally became the Baby Boom, and its members became the Baby Boomers. The next generation, at forty-six million in the United States, was much smaller than the Baby Boomers. It was named Generation X, a name older than the cohort's actual birthdates (c. 1965–1981) but a fitting placeholder for people for whom the stage remained crowded with Boomers. The default name for the next generation, following the alphabet, was Generation Y, but their coming-of-age in the year 2000 suggested the more common tag "Millennials." (Their successors, Generation Z, are called the iGens to emphasize their technology-centered era.)

The ascendance of the scientific method, especially in the West, long ago fostered a habit of relentless research and classification, and the study of "generations" has been a favorite subject. William Strauss and Neil Howe's monumental *Generations*, published in 1991, reaches all the way back to 1584 to develop a theory of four-part generational cycles in America. Generations study other generations, and they study themselves, in search of their defining characteristics, their causes, and their effects. The sheer size and presumed common experience of the Baby Boomers made this effort at identification and explanation an enduring central feature of conversation in the United States, from parlor games to PhD dissertations. They look back and call their parents the "Greatest Generation"; they look forward at their children or grandchildren, the Millennials, often with more mixed emotions. Joel Stein's *Time* magazine cover article on May 20, 2013, reflects the ambivalence: "The Me Me Me Generation: Millennials Are Lazy, Entitled Narcissists Who Still Live With Their Parents. Why

They'll Save Us All."

Many of their managers in the business world stop at the "lazy, entitled narcissists" part. Kids these days have no work ethic, these elders say. They spend too much time on their cell phones. They waste their time playing video games. They're not willing to pay their dues, like the managers did, and the manager's dad and granddad from the Industrial Revolution back through the Agricultural Revolution. Training in "soft skills"—how to show up for work on time, how to dress for success, how to work on a team—has become a cottage industry as their bosses seek to remediate them and tool them to fit an economic engine whose own future is deeply in doubt.

Beyond the workplace, many older people feel an unsettled shock at the decisive break they see from "traditional values." Every generation considers itself rebellious, and every older generation certainly considers the younger generation rebellious. But the Millennials' shift is seismic on a wide range of fronts: dating and marriage across racial lines, motherhood without marriage, promotion of gay rights and same-sex marriage, abandonment of religion, flouting of tradition. Attitudes and behavior once considered fringe have become mainstream, and unlike the Boomers after their own 1960s fling, Millennials as a whole do not appear likely to revert to the mean when they "grow up" to take on the responsibilities of a spouse and kids, a house, and a job. The hierarchical superstructure of society and the reverence for an imagined wholesome past seem unlikely to attract a generation that takes a more egalitarian, dynamic world for granted.

Yet even such an observation calls for nuance and exception. Millennials are not to be generalized as were the Greatest Generation or the Baby Boomers, who have in common significant historical events—Depression, World War II, and Cold War, respectively—or as Gen Xers, the place-holding heirs to Baby Boomers who still cling to the spotlight (Bill Clinton was the first one elected president, and Hillary Clinton could be the last). The accuracy of those old generalizations, beyond a certain racial and economic demographic, is itself open to question, although the generally shared values of those who held political and social power is more clear. In any case, Millennials are not defined by such shared history. Their name is a number, Earth's second thousandth trip around the sun in the Common Era. That accident of history is in some ways all they have as a common identification, precisely because the previous generations set the stage for myriad opportunities and diverse outcomes—ending the Cold War, unleashing technology, establishing self-determination for former colonies and civil rights for onetime second-class citizens. The static world of Plato and the mechanical world of Newton vanished in the face of the dynamism of evolutionary biology, quantum physics, and innovative entrepreneurship. "Everything changes except change," as Heraclitus said, and such is the world of the Millennials.

This, then, is not an attempt to describe "the Millennials" as a group. In this case, certainly, generalizations are never accurate. Sometimes the evidence shows a preponderance of unity on a given topic, sometimes not. This is not an attempt to give you the secret to managing "them" at work or conversing with "them" at parties. No thesis is defended. The individuals who tell their stories here are not occasions for extrapolation or examples of anything beyond themselves. Rather, this is an attempt to describe the environment where Millennials grew up and the environment where we all live—an environment of ideas and technology that, instead of shaping human beings into a single mold, invites and empowers them to shape themselves personally and individually, in substantial and apparently unprecedented ways. The plethora of potential connections and choices is open to far greater numbers of people than before, and the consequences of choosing differently from others may be more positive than negative for the first time. A higher percentage of Millennials than earlier generations may grasp and enact those choices, but they are not in themselves generation-specific.

Much of the reporting in this book focuses on Millennials in the United States, if only because of the greater quantity of accessible data, but the ideas and tools it describes are more or less present around the globe and having their impact on this generation and others. Indeed, the technological potential for international connection is a prominent feature of the modern environment, and an unexpected boom of

Internet connectivity around the globe in recent years is accelerating the potential for information access, person-to-person communication, and individualized self-understanding that is common among Millennials in the United States. Facebook and Twitter were tools of the Arab Spring, and YouTube made a Korean musician named Psy a star around the globe at a level unimaginable in the days of only radio and TV.

Whoever you are, wherever you are, however old you are, this book is about the world where you live now. It is about how that world, with its rich and diverse difference from older worlds, has come to be. I hope it helps you to better understand that world, the people who share it with you, and maybe even yourself. I hope that this story will boost your hope, as it does mine, that the world is on course to a better future with the rising generation.

Chapter 3

THE PAST

Every generation, like every individual, is an extension of humanity into history. It is generated, not self-generating, although it actively influences the world of its time, bequeaths an altered environment to its children, and even impacts the memory of earlier history. It shares the present with the past generations and, eventually, the future generations. It inherits and reinvents, selects and arranges available elements in the world—intellectual and psychological as well as physical and practical—to fashion new combinations, new tools, new realities. In this dynamic interaction, the generation both is shaped by its context and shapes that context for itself and for the future. It is limited by the resources it finds in that context—until it fashions new resources from innovative applications or new discoveries. Untold generations traveled on land no faster than the speed of the horse before the steam engine and the internal combustion engine (never mind that in 1830 a horse beat an early steam locomotive that broke down during the first race challenge); untold generations died of infectious diseases before vaccines and antibiotics; untold generations imagined the world circumscribed by their own community until the telegraph, the telephone, the television, and the Internet transcended distance for human communication.

Much of history, as narrated by most human communities, moves as a series of "defining moments," large-scale events or widespread disruptions such as war, plague, economic depression, or colonization. Those events define eras and generations, at least within the societies where they occur. In premodern times, before global transportation and communication, local markers occurred mostly without reference to each other even during the same time period. Western Europe's Dark Ages, for example, occurred in parallel with the flourishing of the Tang dynasty in Asia and the Islamic Caliphate in North Africa, Iberia, and the Middle East. By the twentieth century, far-flung interconnections elevated the global impact of local events. The assassination of an archduke in Serbia triggered a war that killed more than sixteen million people, including thousands from the United States, Canada, India, Australia, and New Zealand, a disaster whose survivors were called the Lost Generation. Within thirty years, including a global Great Depression, war flared again, killing more than sixty million people—2.5 percent of the world population. Americans, looking back, named the people who endured the Depression and defeated the Axis Powers "the Greatest Generation," and the skyrocketing population growth when they came home "the Baby Boomers." Millennials in the United States are largely the grandchildren of the early Boomers or children of the late Boomers, which means that even within their cohort they experienced significantly different kinds of upbringing. Those parents and grandparents grew up in a time of extraordinary change in the United States and the world. Many of those changes cascaded from the experience of World War II—from the economic impact of unprecedented industrial mobilization and innovation, repurposed for consumer and peacetime applications, to the social and political impact of revulsion to Hitler's inhumanity, unleashing movements for colonial independence around the globe and the Civil Rights Movement in the United States. At the same time, the war revealed the unprecedented power of nuclear weapons, and its end left former Allied Powers, now NATO and the Warsaw Pact plus China, in the tense ideological standoff called the Cold War. These postwar events shaped the world of the Millennials' parents and grandparents and, therefore, the attitudes and assumptions of the environment where they grew up.

Three years after the end of World War II, as part of the humanitarian reaction to Hitler, the new United Nations issued a

Universal Declaration of Human Rights with no nation dissenting. The thirty-article document was unprecedented for its global consensus on the intrinsic value of the individual, as drafting subcommittee Hernán Santa Cruz of Chile wrote:

> *I perceived clearly that I was participating in a truly significant historic event in which a consensus had been reached as to the supreme value of the human person, a value that did not originate in the decision of a worldly power, but rather in the fact of existing—which gave rise to the inalienable right to live free from want and oppression and to fully develop one's personality.*

The declaration codified the world's commitment to avoid ever repeating the horrors of the war just ended, and the strategy elevated the rights of persons above the interests of states that aimed to submerge individuals and oppress other groups. Its language recognizably echoes the U.S. Declaration of Independence, but its drafting deliberately resisted the enshrinement of a particular culture's values, as Eleanor Roosevelt, the chair of the committee, recalled a debate among Charles Malik of Lebanon, John Humphrey of Canada, and Peng Chung Chang of China:

> *Dr. Chang was a pluralist and held forth in charming fashion on the proposition that there is more than one kind of ultimate reality. The Declaration, he says, should reflect more than simply Western ideas and Dr. Humphrey would have to be eclectic in his approach. His remark, though addressed to Dr. Humphrey, was really directed at Dr. Malik, from whom it drew a prompt retort as he expounded at some length the philosophy of Thomas Aquinas. Dr. Humphrey joined enthusiastically in the discussion, and I remember that at one point Dr. Chang suggested that the Secretariat might well spend a few months studying the fundamentals of Confucianism!*

The same impetus in the postwar world led to the independence of former European colonies—more than fifty nations in Africa and more than twenty in Asia. National self-determination was understood as the appropriate arena for personal self-determination. The subjugation by European nations of non-European national groups, accelerated in the late fifteenth century, had reached its peak less than a century earlier, but it was abruptly deemed unacceptable. If the individuals in nations were equal to individuals in other nations, then they had the same right to govern themselves as the people in those nations. There could be no second-class countries, just as there could be no second-class citizens. From its original 51 members, the United Nations grew to 193, adding 16 African nations in 1960 alone. The Roman Catholic Church's Second Vatican Council in the mid-1960s recognized and endorsed this awakening of equality, dignity, the elevation of individual personhood, and a dynamic, evolving human community.

In the United States, where African Americans had been second-class citizens for centuries under slavery and segregation, the Civil Rights Movement accelerated on both governmental and grassroots fronts. President Truman desegregated the military in 1948, the Supreme Court outlawed "separate but equal" Jim Crow laws in 1954, and Congress passed the Civil Rights Act of 1964 and the Voting Rights Act of 1965 as well as a constitutional amendment banning the poll tax that some states had used to prevent African Americans from voting. Meanwhile, the seamstress and NAACP leader Rosa Parks provoked a strike against segregated bus ridership in Montgomery; Freedom Riders crisscrossed the South to demand integrated bus transportation; sit-ins won shared lunch counters; and the Rev. Martin Luther King, Jr. led the March on Washington where he delivered his "I Have a Dream" speech in 1963. Mandated integration of schools and public facilities brought African Americans and Caucasians into a new kind of contact that, despite resistance in many quarters, quickly revealed their common humanity and the sham of the artificial system that kept them apart. The movement provided a template for other groups, including women, people with disabilities, and gays and lesbians to pursue real legal and social equality.

A significant political impetus for U.S. promotion of the Civil Rights Movement was the Cold War. The Soviet Union, chief antagonist in that long standoff based on the "mutually assured destruction" (MAD) of nuclear warheads, delighted in highlighting the hypocrisy of American claims to equality when it relegated a whole race to second-class citizenship. The Cold War was the defining feature of the Baby Boomer generation, just as the Depression and World War II had marked their parents'. The world was bipolar not only geographically, North and South, but politically, East and West. Fear of nuclear destruction in a final battle between the Free World and Communism dominated the world of early Boomers, who laughably were trained to hide under their school desks in case of atomic attack. Many of those children grew up to hold serious debates in college about the advisability of bringing children into such a world.

The black-and-white, with-us-or-against-us either-or of the Cold War organized life for Boomers and their children. Few were old enough to remember the McCarthy hearings in the 1950s; more were gripped by the Cuban Missile Crisis in 1962 and Lyndon Johnson's 1964 "Daisy" campaign ad with its nuclear explosion; none could miss the Doomsday Clock. Scientists set the clock, a graphic warning of nuclear disaster, at 11:53 p.m. in 1947. It reached 11:58 in 1963 and was at 11:57 in the mid-1980s. Congress rushed to add "under God" to the Pledge of Allegiance in the 1950s in the face of godless Communism, just as some states rushed to add the Confederate battle flag to their state flags in the face of desegregation orders. The Soviet launch of Sputnik in 1957 triggered a space race—a one-on-one contest between the United States and the Soviet Union—that culminated in the first moonwalk in 1969.

Unlike their fathers, who marched dutifully to Korea in the early 1950s when the Cold War flared hot, many of the Boomers resisted a repeat in the escalated Vietnam War in the mid-1960s. Many volunteered and more were drafted, but a significant number—raised in the context of at-least-theoretical universal human rights, actual decolonization around the world, and the ongoing Civil Rights Movement—staged protests, burned their draft cards, and fled to

Canada. An estimated thirty to forty thousand people emigrated, and at least another twenty-five thousand who burned their draft cards went unpunished while few were prosecuted.

The peace movement and Civil Rights Movement, focused on the rights of others, occurred in the context of an accelerating focus on the individual's own right to personal self-expression. Supreme Court decisions in the early 1960s outlawed government-sponsored prayer and Bible reading in public schools on the basis of equal protection for other religions and those without religion. *Griswold v. Connecticut* in 1965 established a constitutional right to privacy as it overturned a state ban on contraceptives—just as "the Pill," approved in 1960, was becoming popular. The unleashing of "free love," with its attendant drugs and rock and roll, and Woodstock in 1969 as its icon, became the mythic lore of the '60s, but it was in no way sustained by the vast majority of the Boomers who experienced it. Bill Clinton famously denied having inhaled when he smoked marijuana. Untold Boomers, far from considering the era a worthy bequest for their children, denied their involvement in the drug-and-sex scene or described it with remorse, warning the Xers and Millennials away from its excesses.

All through the 1960s, violent race riots convulsed American cities despite the nonviolent leadership of King, including at least 125 riots in reaction to his assassination in the spring of 1968. President Johnson, facing defeat because of the unpopular war, chose not to seek reelection. The assassination of Robert Kennedy echoed the assassination of his brother President John Kennedy in 1963, and violent suppression of widely televised protests at the Democratic Convention in Chicago deepened disillusionment. The early Xers were just starting school when Richard Nixon was elected president, and by the time Woodstock and the moonwalk were finished, the '60s passed into their parents' rather mythic lore. Their formative years would come in a very different decade.

The postwar economy that had flourished while the Baby Boomers were growing up suffered a major shock when energy costs skyrocketed as a result of an embargo by the Organization of Petroleum Exporting Countries following Israel's defeat of Arab nations in a brief

1973 war. The overall consumer price index rose from 38.8 in 1970 to 96.5 in 1982 and kept escalating steadily. Energy costs accelerated even faster, from a Consumer Price Index of 26.5 in 1971 to 99.2 in 1982. Gasoline rationing and long lines at the pump were the early warning of a deep and broad preoccupation with energy—as an economic, not an environmental, issue. Gas prices jumped from $0.36 a gallon in 1972 to $1.31 a gallon in 1981. The issue became chronic and reached deeply into ordinary life. Speed limits that had been 70 mph or higher were set at 55 mph, architects designed homes and commercial buildings for maximum insulation and minimum heat loss, and President Carter, wearing a sweater, lectured the nation on lowering the thermostat in winter.

The Sunbelt, from the Carolinas to southern California, became a sought-after destination for company relocations that brought unprecedented nonfarm employment, especially to the Old Confederacy. Texas and Arizona added twice as many people in the 1970s as in the previous decade, Alabama three times as many, New Mexico and Mississippi four times as many. In many areas, the number of transplanted Yankees, now officially welcomed for their economic impact, made significant demographic differences.

The 1980 presidential election was the first in which all Boomers were qualified to vote, partly because of a constitutional amendment in 1971 that lowered the voting age to eighteen nationally, and their votes were evenly divided between Ronald Reagan and Jimmy Carter. The election was also a significant marker in the rise of the Religious Right, the Moral Majority led by the Rev. Jerry Falwell. Although Carter, a Southern Baptist, had been frank about his born-again religious experience—once telling *Playboy* magazine that he had, in fact, committed adultery in his heart—Reagan won the backing of organized religious conservatives. The 1973 *Roe v. Wade* Supreme Court decision legalizing abortion had not been a significant issue in the 1976 election between Carter and Gerald Ford, but Reagan embraced opposition to abortion so thoroughly that, at the Republican convention in 1980, George Bush had to announce his newfound "pro-life" stance in order to become the vice presidential candidate.

Heightened engagement by evangelical Protestants and conservative Catholics, many of them previously part of the Democratic coalition, became a standard feature of national elections, focused first on the issue of abortion and then also on the issue of gay rights, especially same-sex marriage. The movement had roots in the late 1970s when Phyllis Schlafly managed to halt the progress of the Equal Rights Amendment for women and Anita Bryant led initiatives to pass laws discriminating against homosexuals.

The country in 1980 was still mired in the energy crisis, exacerbated by the hostage standoff with Iran, and Carter was defeated by Reagan, at sixty-nine the oldest president ever elected. He was inaugurated as the first Xers were coming of age and the early Millennials were being born. During his two terms, he rolled back some of the economic policies of the New Deal and Great Society—especially the level and distribution of taxes—and revived the confrontational rhetoric of the Cold War, labeling the Soviet Union as the Evil Empire. During his second term, the 1986 Supreme Court decision *Bowers v. Hardwick* affirmed the right of states to criminalize homosexual activity. An extension of opportunity for ratification of the Equal Rights Amendment, which once had thirty-five of the required thirty-eight states, expired in 1982. However, legislative efforts to enact a constitutional amendment banning abortion, to overcome *Roe v. Wade*, failed.

In addition to cultivating the religious right, Reagan pursued the Southern Strategy pioneered by Nixon, capitalizing on the unpopularity of Johnson's 1964 Civil Rights Act among Southern whites to win them from the Democrats. To Nixon's code words "law and order" and "states' rights," Reagan added "welfare queen" and attacks on food stamps and affirmative action. The politicizing of the racial division reached a peak in the 1988 election, when George Bush (whose running mate, Dan Quayle, was the first Baby Boomer on a presidential ticket) ran ads focused on Willie Horton, a black man who attacked a Maryland couple and raped the woman after he did not return to jail from furlough under a program in Massachusetts when Michael Dukakis was governor. Bush was elected.

The first Millennials were entering elementary school when the Cold War ended in 1989. The feature that had organized so much of their parents' and grandparents' lives disappeared, virtually overnight, symbolized by the fall of the Berlin Wall. President Bush declared a "new world order," and two years later, the rapid victory in the Persian Gulf War—televised like a high-tech video game—appeared to confirm U.S. hegemony as its one-on-one adversary, the Soviet Union, shattered into Russia and individual independent nations, from the Baltic States to Georgia and Ukraine. Bush's approval ratings soared to nearly 90 percent, but the next year, he was defeated by the first Baby Boomer president, Bill Clinton, whose vice president, Al Gore, was from the same generation. The end of the Cold War and Bush's war victory had made foreign policy far less important than in previous elections. The country was in an economic recession, and the patrician Bush—who publicly marveled at grocery store scanning technology—seemed out of touch. Bush relied on his generation's willingness to take on a "mission"—the same failed appeal of Bob Dole in 1996—and admitted discomfort with "the vision thing."

As a Boomer, Clinton was subjected to questions about drug use in his past, and rumors of adultery were so frequent that they came to be known as "bimbo eruptions." He admitted smoking marijuana but insisted that he didn't inhale, a parsing that also showed up in the second term when he claimed that he "didn't have sex" with Monica Lewinsky. His campaign included playing saxophone on the Arsenio Hall Show, and he later answered a question about his underwear preferences on MTV. Clinton governed differently from previous Democratic presidents, pushing for a North American Free Trade Agreement and "ending welfare as we know it," requiring recipients to move toward employment.

Although Clinton had promised to lift the ban on gays in the military, he compromised with a policy of "don't ask, don't tell," and in 1996 he signed the Defense of Marriage Act in anticipation that some states might eventually legalize same-sex marriage. His opponent for reelection in the 1996 elections was Senator Bob Dole, who appealed for one last turn for his Greatest Generation. Clinton won easily. As the early Millennials were in high school, Clinton's impeachment trial included detailed descriptions of oral sex and a national conversation on what technically constitutes "sex." He was acquitted of the charges of perjury and obstruction of justice in 1999, but the next year, his vice president, Al Gore, lost a close and controversial election to George W. Bush.

The 9/11 attacks on the World Trade Center and the Pentagon, eight months after Bush became president, defined his two terms. He attacked Afghanistan, which was harboring the terrorist mastermind Osama bin Laden, in 2001. Two years later, he attacked Iraq, where he claimed Saddam Hussein—still in power a decade after Bush's father defeated him in Kuwait—was developing weapons of mass destruction. Although both wars extended beyond Bush's eight years in office, they were not the organizing principle of American society at the level of the Great Depression, World War II, and the Cold War. Early comparison of the 9/11 attacks to Pearl Harbor were quickly abandoned, and the "War on Terror" was recognized as a novel, even metaphorical, use like "War on Drugs" or "War on Poverty" because the enemy was not a state. Americans had not been drafted into the military since 1973, and the all-volunteer army engaged a fraction of the population, most of them from lower economic classes. By the time of the attack, as the first Millennials were beginning to enter military service, diversity in the ranks was dramatically increasing. Minorities among officers had grown from 10.5 percent in 1995, to 18.8 percent by 2000, and the minority share of enlisted soldiers leapt from 28.2 percent in 1995 to 38.2 percent in 2000. Hispanics had grown to 10 percent of the enlisted, but African Americans accounted for twice as many men and more than three times as many women. By 2013, however, the percentage of minorities among enlisted had fallen to 32.4 percent, although the percentage of officers had reached 22.4 percent. The 9/11 attack, and especially its subsequent suspension of air travel, triggered a brief recession, but the GDP fully recovered in the following year. Unemployment still had yet to fully recover. In 2000, the average unemployment rate was 4 percent, but rose to a whopping 9.6 percent in 2010. Things seem to be leveling out, as the rate lowered to 6.2 percent by 2014 and continued to drop. As of June 2015, the year's average rate held firm at 5.5 percent.

The war in Iraq was already unpopular by the time of the 2004 election, when the age group eighteen to twenty-nine—including the oldest Millennials—supported John Kerry over George W. Bush by 54 percent to 45 percent. Bush had made privatization of Social Security a campaign theme, but although Millennials feared that the program would be used up by their elders before their own retirement, they did not back such a radical change. On the question of gay rights, the U.S. Supreme Court in 2003 had overturned its *Bowers v. Hardwick* decision and affirmed the right of same-sex couples to privacy, and the Massachusetts Supreme Court that same year had ruled that same-sex couples have a right to marry. Eleven states put constitutional amendments to ban same-sex marriage on their November ballots, and thirteen states banned the arrangement in some form, a move widely credited with energizing turnout that worked to Bush's favor in Ohio and other states.

In 2008, Barack Obama became the first African American and, by most measures, the first Generation X president. Millennials, who registered and voted at about the same rates as Boomers at their age, supported Obama by 66 percent to 32 percent over John McCain. Just before the election, a financial and real estate collapse triggered the worst economic recession in the United States since the Great Depression, at the point when many Millennials were graduating from college and entering the workforce and many Boomers were approaching retirement age. The recovery was slow, with almost all of its benefits going to the wealthiest 1 percent. Obama led a repeal of "don't ask, don't tell" and refused to defend the Defense of Marriage Act, which was struck down by the Supreme Court in June 2013 in *United States v. Windsor.* Although that ruling did not establish a constitutional right to same-sex marriage, three federal circuit courts cited it as they overturned state bans, and in October 2014, the Supreme Court refused to hear appeals of those rulings. That led to the legalization of same-sex marriage in thirty-six states plus the District of Columbia, where 70 percent of Americans live. When the Sixth

Circuit upheld state bans, leading to a division among the lower courts, the Supreme Court agreed to resolve the issue. It heard arguments in the consolidated case, *Obergefell v. Hodges*, in April 2015 and ruled, 5–4, that same-sex marriage was a right nationwide in June 2015.

Until the economic collapse of 2008, Millennials grew up in an almost-constantly expanding economy, with only occasional, brief downturns. They were born after the much deeper recession of the Carter administration, with its stagnant economy and soaring interest rates. Promising new Internet technologies in the 1990s drove stock prices artificially high for some online-heavy companies, the so-called Dot-Com Bubble from 1993 to 2000 that largely collapsed within a year. Some companies such as Amazon survived, and the burst of activity broadened and deepened Internet infrastructure. That collapse did not trigger such widespread economic damage, and it did not interrupt the acceleration of technology itself. As the year 2000 approached, and the early Millennials were in high school, experts of an older generation warned of an impending computer crisis—the Millennium Bug or Y2K—where they expected conventional computer two-digit dating system to crash systems as the date turned over to 00. One book on the subject, published in 1984, was titled *Computers in Crisis,* and the U.S. military spent $2 billion to prepare for "the El Nino of cyberspace," as Deputy Defense Secretary John Hamre called Y2K. Compared to the scale of fear, very few problems actually resulted—whether because of adequate preparation or overestimation of the threat—and nearly everyone woke up on New Year's Day with technology intact. The episode affirmed the reliability and permanence of a feature of Millennial life that would shape their generation's world like wars had shaped their parents'.

Chapter 4

TECHNOLOGY

The most prominent feature of the world where Millennials grew up was not a hot or cold war, a Great Depression, or any other geopolitical circumstance. Instead, ever-accelerating developments in technology—computers, communication, data mining, entertainment, social media, and others—have shaped both their personal and their public environments. While their parents and grandparents marvel at the unprecedented speed and ease of personal contact, information gathering and dissemination, widespread opinion sharing, and on-demand entertainment, Millennials take the technologies for granted and assume that they will perpetually improve. Consider what they have witnessed. In 1998, Nielsen's Law predicted that average household download speed would increase 50 percent every year—and that has, for the most part, held true. From the mid-1990s to 2015, average U.S. household download speed increased from 56 kbps, to 36.4 mbps—a jump of 64,900 percent! The exploding capacity has enabled growth in cloud sharing, mobile devices, and big data. Moore's law similarly predicts that microprocessor technology doubles performance every two years—a 1960s estimate that has become an understatement as inventions and discoveries accelerate.

Such rapid and disruptive change on the basis of technology may have occurred at such periods as the Agricultural Revolution and the Industrial Revolution, but they did not impact the lives of individuals in the same way as the Technological Revolution has affected Millennials. Such earlier technology advancements, if anything, concentrated power in the hands of a few—the owner of the means of production, whether fields or factories—to the detriment of the many. Some new technology-based tools, from the iron plow to the internal combustion engine, supported the feudal system and serfdom (or slavery) in agriculture-based economies and the wide gap between capital and labor in manufacturing ones (described by Charles Dickens and Upton Sinclair, among others). When the Information Age succeeded the Industrial Age in the twentieth-century West, it remained a description of unequal power held by those with the information. Secret formulas for, say, constructing nuclear weapons, as well as closely guarded scientific discoveries or marketing research, could be acquired only at great cost, if at all, and the possessor of such knowledge was the clear superior.

The arc of technological development has bent away from that model to a democratization of information—and power. Technology has made possible new ways to access information, entertainment, news, and technology itself, compounding the speed of change. Open access publications, software, and hardware, as well as online newspapers, blogs, magazines, and music, broaden availability and enable highly individualized selectivity. Although they are available only to those with Internet access, increasingly economical hardware and software along with cheap or free connectivity have dramatically increased that number, and the barrier is far lower than the cost of exclusive proprietary information. Around the world, 2.9 billion new Internet users have been added from 1993 to 2014, raising the total from 0.3 percent of the global population to 40.4 percent. In the United States, the number of users rose from 43 percent in 2000 to 86.75 percent by 2014, though the percentage of users in the United States shifted from 29.65 percent to 9.58 percent, respectively, of all global users. Cell phone usage has also jumped. In a 2014 survey, 98 percent of U.S. Millennials had cell phones, which had grown so common that large majorities of every generation owned them, including more than three-fourths of those older than sixty-five. But 85 percent of Millennials had smartphones, far more than the 79 percent of Xers, 54 percent of Boomers and 27 percent of older people. Virtually all of the personal, mobile, and broad-accessibly changes wrought by technology have occurred within the lifetime of Millennials.

The emergence of computer technology after World War II did not at first contemplate devices for individual users. In the 1960s, when computers were institutional, mainframe, and room-sized, experts at the Rand Corporation estimated that the world would need between seven and nine of them to meet its computing needs. Baby Boomers Steve Jobs and Bill Gates (both born in 1955) introduced the personal computer, enabling individual, at-home, desktop use. Widespread commercial versions of the equipment were developed in the late 1970s, but software to enhance utility did not become available until the early 1980s. In 1982, as the first Millennials were born, *Time* magazine proclaimed the computer "Machine of the Year."

Millennials have never lived in a world without personal computers. Tools are commonplace that were the subject of science fiction or Dick Tracy comic strips for their parents and grandparents. The equipment has evolved from the slow, clunky desktop—not only has desktop capacity and power increased, but handheld devices are vastly more powerful than early desktops. One gigabyte of hard drive space was breaking news for a desktop in 1995, with processing speed of 33 megahertz and 8 megabytes of RAM. The iPhone 6 has up to a 128-gigabyte hard drive, 1.5 gigahertz of processing speed, and 1 gigabyte of RAM. Moreover, by 2015, Apple had introduced a wristwatch that includes GPS, Bluetooth, Wi-Fi, and health-monitoring sensors.

Close on the heels of the at-home computing and word processing capability came the Internet, widely commercialized before the first Millennials reached high school, with its capacity for access and connection beyond the home. Like computers, the Internet began as a cumbersome, slow tool, with dial-up modems that interfered with telephone service and could take hours to download large files. By the late 1990s, cable modems appeared, and broadband was widely employed by 2004.

As the technology has expanded, groups including the U.S. State Department have recognized that Internet freedom is an aspect of the universal rights of freedom of expression and the free flow of information. In early 2015, the Federal Communications Commission decided to regulate broadband Internet service as a public utility, preserving the principles of net neutrality. As the U.S. State Department says:

> *The Internet and other digital technologies enable an unprecedented level of communication and connection among individuals. They empower people across the world with the tools to share ideas and information as never before. In many ways, the Internet is the largest collaborative effort humankind has ever seen, magnifying the power and potential of individual voices on a global scale. Yet just as people use these technologies to express themselves and advance freedom worldwide, numerous governments seek to deny the rights they enable. Repressive regimes are censoring search results, jailing journalists and activists, and imposing laws that restrict online discourse and access to information. Threats to Internet freedom are growing in number and complexity. The State Department not only works to combat Internet censorship, but to ensure the safety of communication and access to information on the new terrain of the twenty-first century.*

Along with political freedom, many have championed lower economic barriers to Internet access. The rise of the Open Source Initiative in 1998 and Creative Commons in 2001 accelerated the development of the Internet and deepened the public presumption that it should remain universally accessible. Linux and Ubuntu operating systems enabled individuals and companies to function without the high cost of proprietary systems such as Microsoft Windows. Free access to scientific research reports, such as the Public Library of Science, in some cases is replacing high-subscription journals. In 2008, the National Institutes of Health decided to require researchers who get federal grants to deposit their manuscripts into a peer-reviewed journal where they will be publicly available within a year of publication.

Advances in technology, especially computer power and Internet connectivity, have reached into virtually every aspect of life. They have brought into the home, even onto the individual person, resources that once required leaving the home to be physically present at libraries, movie theaters, banks, and in some cases even doctors' offices, car repair shops, and workplaces. The breadth of technology's impact covers entertainment, social relationships, work, education, and even health.

ENTERTAINMENT

Television supplanted their parents' radio as a prominent at-home entertainment for the Baby Boomers, but its basic one-directional programming format and passive use remained unchanged until around the birth of the early Millennials. In the United States, the dominance of the Big Three networks—CBS, ABC, and NBC—began to erode in the late 1970s, but the cascade of competing channels made possible by cable and satellite accelerated as the Millennials were growing up. Between 1980 and 2014, approximately 26.4 million viewers completely stopped tuning into these networks' news programs. At the same time, technology for at-home movie viewing provided an alternative to the theaters that had been the only way to view film since its invention at the turn of the twentieth century. Video Home System (VHS) tapes, invented in the 1970s, were popular by the time the first Millennials were born, but they were only the beginning of a rapid sequence of change. DVDs appeared in the United States in the late 1990s, while those children were in high school, and replaced VHS within a decade. The last major motion picture released on VHS was *The History of Violence* in 2006, and production of the cassettes ceased in 2008, although recording and playing devices are still in use. By then, Sony's Blu-ray had begun to supplant the DVD. The standard DVD is 4.7 GB, or up to 8.7 GB in a double-layered version, compared to the standard Blu-ray that holds 25 GB of information, with dual-layer versions capable of holding 50 GB. By 2010, advances in Internet technology allowed streaming video to compete with discs. The disc-distributing giant Netflix, whose business had made it a major user of the U.S. Postal Service, quickly became a major user of the Internet when it introduced subscriptions to streaming videos. Success invites competition, and other companies jumped on the digital bandwagon, offering everything from rentals, to high-definition media streams of movies and TV shows. Now even user-submitted videos, like those on YouTube, can equal or surpass the quality of DVDs. The longstanding practice of cable companies' bundling their offerings in expensive packages began to unravel in late 2014, when HBO and CBS announced that they too would offer stand-alone online streaming subscriptions.

Likewise, the phonograph record was the dominant means of listening to self-selected music (rather than radio programming) for generations across the twentieth century—until the lifetime of Millennials. Audiocassette tapes became popular in the 1970s, leading to the ubiquitous Walkman of the 1980s. The Walkman was the first truly portable vehicle for self-selected music, triggering an explosion in cassette tape demand, but their popularity declined in the face of compact discs (CDs), and automakers had stopped installing cassette players as standard equipment by 2010. CDs, introduced in 1979, surpassed vinyl records in 1988 and remained popular into the 2000s. The MP3 format was introduced in 1994 and grew rapidly through the 1990s. The release of the iPod in 2001 accelerated the shift. In the first week of its opening in 2003, Apple's digital store, iTunes, sold more than one million songs. That same year, Apple Inc. introduced the third generation of iPod, which weighed less than two CDs and held 7,500 songs. By the end of that year, Apple had sold two million iPods, and twenty-five million songs had been downloaded from iTunes.

Rudimentary video games introduced in the 1970s rapidly grew more sophisticated as computer graphics and processing speed increased. By the late 1990s, several popular computer games like Quake, Half-Life, and Diablo supported online multiplayer capabilities. By the early 2000s, online capabilities were barely being introduced to

gaming consoles, but they have since then thrived, allowing international audiences not only to play games and communicate together but
also to purchase games, stream movies and television shows, and even
browse the Internet.

Older generations grew up in a world where "games" involved
balls, fields, and courts, or at least boards, cards, and dice. The word
meant physical activity with physical stuff, whether indoors or
outdoors. For many of those generations, observing younger people
spending hours at a time in front of a flat-screen, manipulating virtual
objects with a keyboard or joystick, can lead to the conclusion that they
are wasting time—as if they were spending so many hours watching
television in the passive way of their parents and grandparents. But
the activity is significantly different. It is more like active engagement
in reading a book or watching a movie, with the added dimensions of
decision-making, often narrative-directing, involvement in the action,
as well as a high level of hand-eye coordination. The experience has
left many Millennials with instinctive visual-spatial skills far superior
to those of previous generations, including the ability to imagine the
three-dimensionality of objects on a computer screen. Gaming has
also improved hand-eye coordination for surgeons. A 2007 study by
six physicians, "The Impact of Video Games on Training Surgeons in
the Twenty-First Century," concluded:

> *Video game skill correlates with laparoscopic surgical skills.
> Training curricula that include video games may help thin the
> technical interface between surgeons and screen-mediated
> applications, such as laparoscopic surgery. Video games may
> be a practical teaching tool to help train surgeons.*

The study showed that surgeons experienced at video games
worked 27 percent faster, made 37 percent fewer errors, and scored 42
percent better on laparoscopic surgery and suturing drills than those
with no gaming experience. In a later study, the researchers found
that surgeons who warmed up with video games before laparoscopic
suturing also were faster and made fewer errors.

HEALTH CARE AND MORE

Driven by Baby Boomers' refusal to accept their parents' low-activity later years, technology has been leveraged to provide support for a more vigorous life, from hip replacement to sexual performance enhancement. Millennials growing up in this environment can have an expectation, not just a hope, that they will remain healthy and active throughout their lives. Increased access to abundant information and tools to help manage diet, nutrition, exercise, lifestyle illnesses such as smoking, alternative medicines and therapies, and other health topics enable them to engage their personal health more efficiently than those who rely solely on the occasional visit to a medical doctor.

In medicine as in many other fields, Millennials with quick access to extensive information are more likely to demand evidence and take a practical approach, adopting what works rather than accepting the conventional wisdom, received tradition, or expert opinion unquestioned. Millennials are also leveraging technology—specifically gaming—to seek cures. Companies like FoldIt and Fit2Cure were created to enlist thousands of online game players to discover information about protein folding or potential drug targets. Fit2Cure, founded by three graduate students at the University of Notre Dame, aimed to identify potential protein pockets where drugs could attach. "What we need is a new paradigm in health care, a new way to do discovery for drugs," said cofounder Ian Sander, whose game can be likened to *Where's Waldo?*:

> *As you apply more and more people to a problem, the more discoveries you get. This represents a huge potential source of collective intelligence. Knowledge spreads in new ways. We want to make it really easy and really fun for people to engage and try to solve medical problems. This is going to be an explosion of engagement and tools that can scale discovery to a million people.*

EDUCATION

Technology is also democratizing access to higher education. EdX, a massive open online course venture founded in 2012 by Harvard University and the Massachusetts Institute of Technology, grew to a million students within a year, and similar services such as Coursera have flourished offering hundreds of online courses. EdX offers courses from top universities around the world, accessible any time so that students can arrange the study to fit their lifestyle, work, family, and other commitments, and learn at their own pace. The OpenCourseWare Consortium, founded in 2006, assists hundreds of universities around the world whose professors post lectures, in a multitude of formats, for free public access. Several universities publish lecture recordings on YouTube, completely accessible to the general public. Education is more accessible than ever.

WORKPLACE

Much of corporate America, having adopted technology for business uses, initially resisted employees' use of personal devices and blocked access to certain online sites in the name of increasing productivity. By 2014, nearly three-fourths of companies approved personal device use for work, partly because of the explosion of smartphones and tablets as supplements to desktops and laptops. In fact, the presence of such devices in the workplace and the less formal environment in some industries and companies, driven by Millennial-heavy workforces, has led to a positive impact for workers. Companies that explore options such as telecommuting, flextime, and results-only work environments are more attractive to Millennials who want a deeper integration of work and life than their parents and grandparents. Work campuses like Google's have become models by providing convenient free food and drink—often shared among colleagues—as well as work-life integrating policies such as bringing your pet to work, weekly socializing with free beer and wine, free transportation to and from work, concierge services for errands, fitness classes, gyms, intramural sports, and generous maternity leave, time off, and room in your schedule to devote to your personal passion.

Some companies have adopted a policy of permitting their employees to work from home for at least a portion of their jobs. A February 2013 Stanford study estimated that 10 percent of U.S. employees work from home. While many in older generations worry that the practice means "shirk from home," an experiment in a sixteen-thousand-employee Chinese travel agency showed otherwise. Employees were assigned to a group that worked from home or a group that worked from the office. The group that worked from home had a 13 percent performance increase, with fewer breaks and sick days, more calls per minute, less turnover, and more job satisfaction. When the company opened the option to the full staff, more than half opted to work from home.

Technology has also enabled many people to start their own businesses, including people who lost jobs or were unable to find work during the recession that began in 2008. Many laid-off workers formed consulting companies with their former employers, who had decided to outsource the task, as the first customers. Many Millennials, already deferring marriage, took the opportunity to attempt their own start-ups or to participate in meaningful community service jobs or internships. The desire to change jobs or start a new business sometimes might arise from impatience with corporate structures that demand years of repetitive "dues paying" for advancement up a tiered system—the corporate ladder.

SOCIAL LIFE

The same technologies that have equipped businesses to heighten productivity and reach far wider markets have empowered individuals to establish and maintain connections, at least on some level, with a host of people in far-flung places. These connections are not only at their fingertips but in their pockets—they can alert their friends when they are at a local restaurant or bar, and they can send a 140-character message around the world. Keeping in touch with a high school sweetheart or college roommate no longer requires mailing a letter or even catching them on the phone—a text message, email, or online posting will show up for them to find at their leisure and respond at their pleasure. Companies like Skype and Google even provide free voice-over IP (VoIP) services, which allow phone calls to be exchanged over the Internet, or better yet, video calls between both mobile and computer devices. At the same time, all of these connections are personally and preferentially selected—social media, so far from mass media, is completely subject to idiosyncratic individual choice. The release of words or images into cyberspace is a private decision, even if a bad decision leaves those words and images open to unintended viewers. The 24/7 access to such expressions and connections, especially as employers ease workplace restrictions on devices, enhances the work-life integration sought by many Millennials and others.

CONCLUSION

Unprecedented technologies have impacted each area of life and lowered the barriers between those areas—family, friends, work, entertainment, etc.—at levels not widely seen since the rise of the factory and the corporation moved workers away from the family farm and the cottage industry. At the same time, those technologies have provided instant access to information about events in every part of the world and fostered the possibility of relating to virtually anyone anywhere. Such awareness and connection were not available in previous generations. Coupled with the relentless postwar movements for recognition of individual rights and dignity and the shaping of their own highly individualized lifestyles, this knowledge has radically altered many people's understanding of the "other." The expectation that others' lives should look like their own, so common in previous generations, has widely receded. Insistence on a singular "right" way to live has yielded to a far more common embrace of diversity.

Chapter 5

DIVERSITY

Millennials live in an environment shaped by a history of expanding human rights and the modern feature of globalization enabled by accelerating technologies. Contact with people of other races, religions, cultures, ethnic groups, and other differences is more frequent for more people than at any other time in the past. Immigration and travel bring people into geographic proximity, and old structures that otherwise kept them apart—colonization, segregation, apartheid, rigidly ethnic neighborhoods—are in full retreat in most parts of the world. In the United States, government agencies have recognized a widening array of ethnic identities. The 1980 census added "Vietnamese," "Indian (East)," "Guamanian," "Samoan," and "Aleut" to a list that already included "Negro" or "Black," "American Indian," and "Korean" as identification options. That was a far cry from the 1890 census, the first to describe race rather than only color, with the options of "White," "Black," "Mulatto," "Quadroon," "Octoroon," "Chinese," "Japanese," or "Indian." Colleges and universities more than forty years ago started expanding their curriculums beyond the "dead white men" of European philosophers and writers, adding diverse options of gender and ethnic studies. Recognition of important contributions from different cultures and societies has accelerated in a globalized world of scientific and technological research as well as economic trade and instant communication.

Prejudice against the "other" typically involves an abstracted stereotype. The "different" group becomes an imagined mob intent on doing harm, to justify the dominant group's defensive actions. Belgian colonizers in Rwanda created "those Tutsi" and "those Hutu" to keep the conquered people divided. White Southerners in the United States warned against "those blacks" who wanted to "destroy our way of life," and Hispanics, Muslims, and gays have received similar treatment in the twenty-first century in America. Various Hispanic groups are lumped as "Mexicans." A woman at a John McCain campaign stop in 2008 referred to Barack Obama as an "Arab," meaning "Muslim," meaning "terrorist," and McCain won praise for replying, "He's not an Arab. He's a good family man," as if "Arab" and "good family man" were necessarily distinct.

A young girl, Scout Finch, in *To Kill a Mockingbird* disbanded a lynch mob by singling out a man she knew and engaging him as a human being. Harvey Milk, the openly gay member of the San Francisco Board of Examiners, defeated anti-homosexual campaigns by urging gays to reveal their orientation so that friends and family would recognize their common humanity. Government-driven integration of schools, lunch counters, and other public facilities in the United States enabled the development of personal contacts to the same effect. In other nations, various Truth and Reconciliation Commissions advanced national unity after apartheid and genocide. In South Africa, for example, investigations that began in the mid-1990s led to transparent discussion of apartheid-era atrocities and amnesty for 849 people, as well as reparation and rehabilitation for victims. Part of Rwanda's reconciliation involved a local judicial assembly, called Gacaca, that heard testimony and gave perpetrators opportunities to express repentance and reconciliation. Many of the 1.2 million cases tried under this system restored people to their reconciled communities.

The contact afforded by technology, most fully utilized by Millennials, has had the same effect, but far more rapidly, broadly, and deeply. Millennials are far more likely than their parents and grandparents to assign high value to diversity and inclusion, certainly far more than their ancestors were at their age decades ago. In a February 2013 survey of more than 2,700 members of the National

Society of High School Scholars, more than 70 percent listed "respect for differences" as an important quality in relationships, behind only honesty and loyalty. More than half identified "building relationships across different cultures" as what they would like to be known for—the top choice, and far ahead of "being an inventor of new technology" and "becoming a philanthropist."

"Anyone can respect someone they like," said one who listed "respect for others" as a top quality for friendship. "But respecting a person who you may not know at all, or may not even like, shows a strong character."

While most of the students focused on career goals, many aimed for broader impact when asked what they would like to be known for.

"I would most like to be known for bringing humankind together as a whole," one said. "To bring people together no matter their race, age, gender, creed, national origin, sexual orientation would be the most rewarding thing I can imagine."

Others echoed that sentiment:

"Building relationships that aren't centered on cultures, that emphasize that we're all humans, and that we should have to TRY to accept other humans, no matter their color, beliefs, or customs."

"I am more of a STEM-based student, but also understand the importance of cultures and pluralism and would like to help the world accept them as well."

"I would like to be known as a person who used science and technology to unite different cultures and at the same time improve living conditions in poor neighborhoods by giving up my time and effort to build and make organizations and educational centers for the poor and disadvantaged."

This is a far cry from the "melting pot" metaphor that prevailed in the United States from the beginning of the nation until the late twentieth century. Even that image stood for a combination of *Europeans*, particularly northern Europeans, with Asians, Africans, and sometimes Southern Europeans excluded. As J. Hector St. John de Crevecoeur wrote in *Letters from an American Farmer* (1782):

> *What, then, is the American, this new man? He is neither a European nor the descendant of a European; hence that strange mixture of blood, which you will find in no other country. I could point out to you a family whose grandfather was an Englishman, whose wife was Dutch, whose son married a French woman, and whose present four sons have now four wives of different nations. He is an American, who, leaving behind him all his ancient prejudices and manners, receives new ones from the new mode of life he has embraced, the new government he obeys, and the new rank he holds... The Americans were once scattered all over Europe; here they are incorporated into one of the finest systems of population that has ever appeared.*

Nearly a century later, in 1875, Titus Munson Coan wrote in *The Galaxy* magazine:

> *The fusing process goes on as in a blast-furnace; one generation, a single year even, transforms the English, the German, the Irish emigrant into an American. Uniform institutions, ideas, language, the influence of the majority, bring us soon to a similar complexion; the individuality of the immigrant, almost even his traits of race and religion, fuse down in the democratic alembic like chips of brass thrown into the melting pot.*

In 1908, a character in the play *The Melting Pot* declared:

> *Understand that America is God's Crucible, the great Melting-Pot where all the races of Europe are melting and re-forming! Here you stand, good folk, think I, when I see them at Ellis Island, here you stand in your fifty groups, your*

fifty languages, and histories, and your fifty blood hatreds and
rivalries. But you won't be long like that, brothers, for these are
the fires of God you've come to – these are fires of God. A fig for
your feuds and vendettas! Germans and Frenchmen, Irishmen
and Englishmen, Jews and Russians—into the Crucible with
you all! God is making the American.

Ralph Waldo Emerson had proposed a more inclusive melting pot in his journal in 1845, but the text was not published until 1912:

Man is the most composite of all creatures… Well, as in
the old burning of the Temple at Corinth, by the melting
and intermixture of silver and gold and other metals a new
compound more precious than any, called Corinthian brass,
was formed; so in this continent, – asylum of all nations, – the
energy of Irish, Germans, Swedes, Poles, and Cossacks, and all
the European tribes, – of the Africans, and of the Polynesians,
– will construct a new race, a new religion, a new state, a new
literature, which will be as vigorous as the new Europe which
came out of the smelting pot of the Dark Ages, or that which
earlier emerged from the Pelasgic and Etruscan barbarism.

Revulsion to Hitler's policies and the Holocaust accelerated the inclusion of non-Europeans in the American melting pot after World War II—although the nation had forced Japanese Americans into internment camps during the war—as well as the liberation of European colonies around the world. But the image persisted generally until the 1970s, when it began to give way to a "salad bowl," "quilt," or "stew" metaphor that emphasized the persistence of diverse cultures within the American whole. State laws against interracial marriage were struck down by the Supreme Court in *Loving v. Virginia* in 1967.

As practiced by previous generations, beginning with the Civil Rights Movement, diversity in the United States involved legal requirements, such as public facility integration and "affirmative action" to encourage fuller participation of women and minorities in education, government, and business—an effort to achieve greater categorical balance often subject to charges of quotas and tokenism. But for many Millennials who grew up in integrated environments, and whose social media connections span the globe, relating to those who are different comes naturally—varieties of race, religion, color, national origin, gender, sexual orientation, etc., appear as incidental as varieties of height, eye color, and hair length.

For generations, dominant groups, especially Europeans, sought to establish their bias against various groups as a reflection of objective reality. Ruling religion and science conspired, for example, to portray Africans as an inferior class—condemned by God to slavery, according to sermons on Genesis 9, and lacking in the cranial capacity of the white race, according to scientists. Millennials grew up in a world where these theories were dramatically debunked, particularly by Stephen Jay Gould's *Mismeasure of Man* published in 1981. Although the academic debate goes on—Richard Herrnstein and Charles Murray's *The Bell Curve* reasserted a genetic basis for intelligence in 1994—popular opinion decisively rejects such classification. Harvard President Lawrence Summers ignited a firestorm when he suggested a gender distinction in science and engineering aptitude in 2005, contributing to a no-confidence vote by the Harvard faculty that led to his resignation.

The accelerated social acceptance of gay rights described above, in particular marriage equality, reflects a broader assumption of the individual's right to choose their own way of life and self-expression. The widespread acceptance of births to single women, now more than half of U.S. births, and the evaporation of the term "illegitimate" for those children that was common just a generation ago, is another example.

The reflexive acceptance of difference apparently is both a cause and a consequence of a larger feature among many Millennials: a rejection of hierarchical structures. Discriminatory identification of supposedly inferior groups historically has been central to organizing society—not only in a caste system such as India's, but even in the supposedly egalitarian United States. The category of second-class citizenship has been central to the retention of White Anglo-Saxon Protestant privilege, but those who defend it have moved from the center to the fringe. Within another generation, Caucasians will no longer hold a population majority in the United States—there will be no majority. While minorities have succeeded in retaining their privilege in many societies for extended periods of time—the racial minority in South Africa, the religious minority in Iraq and Syria—those structures eventually collapse. Nothing of that sort seems likely in the United States, which has already elected an African American president and seated a Hispanic woman on the Supreme Court. The rising generation is far less inclined to relegate any group, as a group, to less-than-equal status.

Heightened awareness of diversity has led to a strong anti-bullying movement in the United States—the inverse of older times when targeting the Other for mistreatment was accepted, even expected. The enthusiasm for games of "smear the queer," the quick hilarity at racist jokes and epithets, the catcalls and propositioning of women in public and in the workplace, the imitative mocking of people with disabilities all fostered presuppositions of the dominant group's superiority. Psychological experiments that became part of *Brown v. Board* indicated that most African American children, given the choice between a black doll and a white doll, said the white doll was nicer—especially if they attended segregated schools. A repeat of the experiment in Harlem in 2005 found the same results. This was an environment where the crayon in the Crayola box marked "Flesh" matched the pinkish Caucasian color from 1949 to 1962, when it was renamed "Peach," and "Indian Red," introduced in 1958, became "Chestnut" in 1999. The first African Americans who attended previously all-white schools were jeered, spat on, and threatened. Stereotypes such as "Amos and Andy" were routinely on television and in commercials. In the 1990s, the popular Cracker Barrel Old Country Store had an official policy against hiring gays and lesbians, and it was found guilty of discriminating against African American and female employees and African American customers. Sexual orientation was added to its nondiscrimination policy in 2002.

Many of these assumptions and practices were under attack and in retreat as the Millennials were growing up. Although he was confirmed to the Supreme Court, Clarence Thomas's trial called attention to harassment of women in the workplace. The brutal murder of Matthew Shepard, a gay man in Wyoming, in 1998 led to hate crime legislation aimed at protecting homosexuals, although the federal Matthew Shepard Act did not become law until 2009. Republican Senator George Allen of Virginia saw his reelection campaign in 2006 collapse after a video went viral that caught him calling a dark-skinned young man "macaca" at a rally, a stunning contrast to the success in the 1980s of Senator Jesse Helms's "white hands" advertisement in North Carolina and George H. W. Bush's Willy Horton advertisement. The suicide of Rutgers University freshman Tyler Clementi in 2010, after his roommate spread a video of Clementi kissing another man, highlighted the problem of cyberbullying that had led to numerous teen suicides. His roommate was convicted and served jail time for his role in the cyberbullying.

In addition to bullying, racial profiling has come under attack as a discriminatory practice. A stop-and-frisk program in New York City targeted African Americans more than half of the time between 2002 and 2012, with Latinos about one-third of the time and whites about 10 percent. Nearly 90 percent of those stopped were innocent of any wrongdoing. In 2013, a federal judge ruled that practice violated the individuals' constitutional rights. In Arizona, a judge found in 2013 that Sheriff Joe Arpaio was guilty of racially and ethnically profiling Latinos. The racial disparity in incarceration rates, marijuana and other drug arrests, death penalties, and other crime-related statistics has called into question the justice of the system. In 2015, numerous reports of unarmed black suspects being killed led to a nationwide focus on race and poverty. The U.S. Justice Department discovered a pattern of racist activity in major U.S. cities and promised reform.

Millennials have grown up in a U.S. society more diverse and more accepting of diversity than any previous generation. Widely publicized demographic projections have concluded that within their lifetimes, the United States will no longer have a single ethnic majority, and the trend is already evident. In 2013, more white Americans died than were born, while minority births nearly equaled the number of Caucasian births. Some white Americans in every age group, including Millennials, have resisted the trend or sought to retain advantages in the face of it. White Republican legislators in some states, for example, have drawn district lines and passed identification requirements to dilute black voting strength. But the general trend is unmistakable, and Millennials have embraced it more enthusiastically than any other generation.

Chapter 6

THE PRESENT

Historical trends and technological advances, particularly in the United States but also around the globe, converged to create an environment for Millennials unlike that of any other generation. For the first time, people in different parts of the world not only could know about each other but also could contact each other instantaneously. For the first time, the "us versus them" paradigm of nation, race, war, or ideology no longer provided the template for self-understanding. For the first time, history was perceived as dynamic rather than static, change as normal, innovation as desirable, and static tradition as unsustainable. For the first time, in the welter of the experience of other lifestyles and the exchange of ideas, no single set of life-organizing ideas—religious, philosophical, political, or economic—set the standard for judging all other possibilities. Even religious identification was changing rapidly, driven by the Millennials who reported no affiliation—the "Nones." Thirty-six percent of individuals between eighteen and twenty-nine years of age were religiously unaffiliated. Fewer than 60 percent of Millennials identified as Christians, compared to the 70 percent of the previous generation.

Few people, if anyone, seriously dispute these changes. Those who regret and resist the new reality are acknowledging it as much as those who celebrate and champion it. Some, especially in the older generations, perceive a grave threat, not only to the old order but to civilization itself. The rhetoric of the opposition to same-sex marriage, for example, is sometimes apocalyptic: These arrangements are being sanctioned for the first time in the history of the human race, signaling the end of "traditional" marriage, "traditional" family, and the only organization that humans have ever known. While every generation has expressed shock bordering on hysteria at the misbehavior of the youth, in this case, the elders are correct. Individual freedoms and alternative choices are, in fact, in the ascendancy, not just among outlier groups but enshrined in legal, institutional norms. Same-sex marriage is only one of numerous fundamental social lines crossed in the lifetime of Millennials: for the first time in the United States, the majority of births are to single women; an African American has been elected president; Muslims and atheists have been elected to the U.S. Congress; states have legalized marijuana; more white Americans died than were born in a full year; the end of majority-race status is documented in sight. These are not changes easily reversed, like the rapid ebbing of the Boomers' 1960s rebellion after the assassination of King and Kennedy and the election of Nixon—when the drugs remained illegal, the responsibilities of two-parent households pressed in, and the children co-opted the music. Millennials are driving much of the change. In 2006, about one-third of Millennials favored legalizing marijuana, about the same percentage as Boomers; by 2015, 68 percent of Millennials favored the change, comparative to the 50 percent of Boomers. Millennials' support for same-sex marriage rose from 51 percent in 2003, to 73 percent in 2015, while Xers' support for same-sex marriage rose from 40 percent to 59 percent during the same years.

The changes commonplace around the maturing Millennials were not exchanges of one singular way of life for another—as, for example, resistance to Communism succeeded resistance to Fascism for an earlier generation. Instead, they were a multiplication, a proliferation of choices—new choices, once-marginalized choices increasingly accepted, and idiosyncratic, eclectic collections tailored to personal taste. The splintering of television from the long-established Big Three to a myriad of cable, satellite, and other outlets can stand for the explosion of personal choices in lifestyle, entertainment, religion (or not), education, household arrangement, cuisine, career, and every other dimension. The ease of these choices was enhanced by the virtually uninterrupted economic boom years from Reagan until the Great Recession, and the stagnation of their early adult lives since then has called into question their parents' obsession with deferring their own economic enjoyment for retirement.

Millennials' choices, for example, include the option for women to stay at home with their children rather than working outside the home, a lifestyle less favored by the norms of late Boomers and Xers. "This is not the same basis as pre-feminist women who stayed at home and took care of kids with no choice," consultant Shaunice Hawkins says. "Some decide to stay in the workforce, some are entrepreneurs with home-based businesses."

Such vast possibility fosters a very different mindset from earlier generations often characterized by necessity—obey the rules, follow your father's footsteps, color within the lines, protect what you have. People who make choices in such an open environment have no reason, like those in previous ages, to question the preferential choices of others. "Do your own thing" was invented in the 1960s, but it has become a reality, not a slogan—the rule, not a sly exception to the rules. Even the ubiquitous "Whatever," often considered an uncaring shrug, can actually communicate a sincere permission and acceptance. Millennials might choose very differently, making assumptions far more out-of-the-box than previous generations. Their apparent large-scale agreement on some issues reflects not their personal behavior but their respect for the different choices of others. Far fewer, one assumes, will practice same-sex marriage than the number that routinely supports it in polls, but the large majority indicates a deep belief in the other's right to be different. Millennials are also more open to changing their minds than earlier generations for whom religious conversion was apostasy and political "flip-flopping" was a cardinal sin.

Previous generations in general had detailed systems of right and wrong, often religiously based. There was a presumption of singularity: "Truth is one," "There's one way to salvation," "Right is right and wrong is wrong." Those codes supported societies of inequality—

clerical/lay, majority/minority, owners/workers, white/nonwhite. People assumed that another's deviance from the code did damage to the society as a whole, and thus to each individual. Hence such features as interracial marriage, same-sex marriage, and immigrants' cultural expressions were considered threats to the social fabric.

Millennials live in an environment that accepts multiplicity and proposes diversity instead of singularity. A high percentage of those in the majority, racially or culturally, easily accept the differences of those in the minority, and vice versa. They are more likely to consult their friendship groups, and those groups are far more likely to include people who are very different from them. A Reuters poll in 2013 found that 40 percent of white Americans had no friends or family members of a different race, but 90 percent of U.S. adults under age thirty had such relationships. Each person is, in a way, both a majority of one and a minority of one, with a complete set of rights to be respected. People understand their own behavior largely as a set of preferential choices, rather than the only absolutely right thing to do, and they consider differing behavior as a set of other preferential choices worthy of respect, rather than an absolute wrong. They reject the hierarchical structure of societies governed by a particular set of rules, including religious strictures. The society's law, in this view, has no place in governing the choices of individuals or mutually consenting adults that are not actually harmful to other people, and the society's mores are merely one set of possible choices among many. They are willing and able to negotiate conduct within their own friendship groups to achieve general satisfaction, and they may chafe at organizational structures, including corporations, that do not take such a democratic view.

Millennials, like all other human beings, continue to make choices in their relationships, to distinguish among those who are close friends, acquaintances, strangers, and even enemies. But a high proportion of them recognize that they are selecting according to their personal preferences and whatever other attraction, or lack, the other individual might possess—not as a member of a group with a certain status but as a person with certain qualities. This self-aware choice does not entail disrespect for those not identified as friends, certainly not the kind of categorical disrespect held for second-class groups. The other's freedom is as clear to the one who makes the choice as their own freedom is.

Unlike the common approach of earlier generations, many Millennials tend to evaluate another's actions without self-reference—"*They* must like doing that" rather than "How would *I* feel in that situation?" An older observer who notices Millennials texting during a talk might mistakenly conclude, "They are not paying attention, because I couldn't do that and pay attention," when in fact the skilled young person is capable of handling both. Likewise, the old rules about relating socially with people from work might not apply to a generation intent on living an integrated life.

In 1986, for example, only 33 percent of Americans considered interracial marriage acceptable for everyone while 28 percent reportedly thought it was not acceptable for anyone. By 2012, 63 percent of Americans said it would be fine with them if a family member intermarried, and 35 percent had a close relative who was married outside their racial or ethnic group. Ninety-three percent of Millennials approved of dating between blacks and whites, above the national average of 83 percent and the oldest generation's 67 percent. Eighty-five percent of Millennials approved of the interracial marriage of a family member, compared to 48 percent of the Silent Generation. About 12 percent of new marriages in 2013 were interracial, a record high.

The unprecedented variety of identity and experience among Millennials can baffle researchers and writers attempting to advance a thesis about them. Characterization can include both "coddled and spoiled" and "independent and self-confident." That's why Stein's *Time* magazine article, "The Me Me Me Generation: Millennials Are Lazy, Entitled Narcissists Who Still Live With Their Parents. Why They'll Save Us All," provoked a firestorm of protest.

"It has less to do with them and more to do with the generation that's evaluating them," says Candace Barnhart, the former-longtime Chief Diversity Officer for Nationwide Insurance. "It has to do with the self-absorbed nature of the Baby Boomers, and I'm one of them. There is sort of a view that somehow the Millennials need to believe what we believe to be true. Their truth is less relevant." The Millennials' view became more relevant, she says, when she discussed the question with a younger coworker who explained: "Somebody needs to get over themselves, but it ain't us. Your pension is in my hands."

Some of the differences among Millennials stem from whether they were born of late Boomers or early Xers, whose parenting styles contrasted.

"There's a difference in the Millennials born of Boomers and the Gen Xers," says longtime diversity consultant Shaunice Hawkins, an Xer whose son and daughter will be grown by the time she's forty-five. "I do see a very significant difference between my colleagues and my friends who have children the same age or three or four years older. Their children are much more independent. They seem to be much more structured. They're a little bit more grounded with regard to their values."

Neil Howe, who has conducted extensive research on Millennials and popularized the term in his 2000 book *Millennials Rising* with William Strauss, agrees.

"There's some interesting differences," he says:

> I think the Xers tend to be more hands-on. They put a lot of emphasis on spending time with their kids. They're more intent on making their kids feel comfortable and at ease with themselves rather than making their kids excel. Xers have repudiated the Supermom effort where women played Mozart tapes to their unborn children. You hear a lot of moms among the Xers talking about the 'good-enough mom.' Xers, who may have been latchkey kids, have more commitment that their children will always have someone looking after them, someone with them.

While parents from both generations can be "helicopter parents," Boomers are more noisy and Xers more stealthy, showing up only at the moment when they file a lawsuit or pull their child from a school, for example.

"We see huge changes in school boards and the politics of local school districts now that the Xer parents are calling the shots," Howe says:

Xers, they're a little bit less likely to be moved by a sense of the common community in the way Boomers still were. You could have gotten Boomers to volunteer by sitting on the curriculum committee. One thing I hear from school systems all the time is that Xers only want to chaperone their own kid's classroom to keep an eye on kids— 'It's got to do something for me.' A lot of their attitude toward school politics is looking out for their own kids' interest. There's less trust, less civic engagement, more of an individualist survival mentality.

Hawkins, like many other Xers, feels sandwiched between the much larger Boomers, who for personal and economic reasons are delaying their move out of the workplace that would make room for her age group, and Millennials, who may take over in a succession that skips a generation.

"We're a much smaller group," she says. "From day one, we're the neglected ones, we're the latchkey kids. Through no fault of their own, Gen Xers are put in a position where Boomers are saying 'We want you to train Millennials; we want you to be their coaches, their mentors.' We personally feel as if we've paid our dues. We have this enormous group of Boomers whom we respect, we admire; we've been coached by them. They aren't moving so that we can have the same growth that they had in their time.

"Millennials are smarter, they're quicker, they're fast. But they're weaker in that they don't live independently. They're very co-dependent. They're very community-based. If something happens with the community, parts of them are lost and they don't recover well."

"Boundaries are blurred," agreed consultant Tanya Odom, a diversity expert and Xer. "Millennials will sacrifice their job before their life. They're bringing in this new perspective. "

That relationship focus puts Millennials in contrast with both Boomers and Xers.

"The Boomer says experience is more important—work hard, be loyal, that will be recognized, earn your way up the ladder," Odom says. "Millennials have a different sense—it's through communal relationships that I move up the ladder. Many of them are leaving to go to smaller companies, smaller places where they can have a big effect. They would prefer not to be a small fish in the bigger pond. They're not interested in the things that Gen Xers have always thought they deserved. It's hard as a Gen Xer, because you see two dynamics going on, and they're frustrated. Corporate boomers value loyalty and are willing to put up with shabby treatment for more money. Millennials are saying 'You can take your loyalty and put it where the sun don't shine. This is about me and my life. It will not be dictated by you. It will be dictated by the community. Guys, should I leave my job? What do you think?'

Howe agrees that workers, especially college-educated ones, are frustrated in most workplaces. "Millennials want something very different from employers," he says:

> *They want teamwork, feedback, and communication with executives and older people. They are less concerned with privacy than previous generations and believe the employer should be taking care of its employees. That's a rapid shift we've seen toward what I call the in loco parentis of employers. Their parents and every other institution has taken care of them.*

> *The perfect employer for Millennials would offer a great deal of variety on the job, but they would never have to go out on the job market. One of the most remarkable trends is the increasing share of Millennials who get their first career jobs after college as a result of an internship. You avoid ever going out on the job market. That's what they aspire to. Of course, they don't always get it.*

Millennials overall, and especially women, have a higher level of education than any previous generation. Twenty-seven percent of Millennial women had at least a bachelor's degree by the time they were thirty-three, compared to only 7 percent of Silent Generation women. Twenty-one percent of Millennial men had at least a bachelor's degree by age thirty-three, compared to 12 percent of Silent Generation men. Because not all Millennials have reached that age, they do not yet lead Gen Xers and Boomers in this category, but they are on track to surpass them eventually. Only 3 percent of Millennial men and 2 percent of Millennial women have achieved less than a ninth grade education. The dynamic nature of the workplace and the ease of access to online learning—courses from leading institutions available for free—are enhancing the potential for constant learning and personal reinvention. At the same time, student loan debt leapt between 2004 and 2015, from $260 billion to nearly $1.2 trillion. By 2010, student loan debt had, for the first time, exceeded credit card debt, which was $740 billion, and auto loan debt at $700 billion. One-third of Millennials surveyed by *Forbes* magazine in 2013 regretted going to college because they were saddled with such high debt. With the economy in its deepest downturn since the Great Depression, those strains hobbled many Millennials' ability to buy homes and start families. The number of borrowers nearly doubled between 2004 and 2014, and average loan balances grew 74 percent, with a median of $14,000.

Much of the reaction to complaints about Millennials blames parenting for the effects. Barnhart says the older generation built the ladder that Millennials want to climb—but the Millennials, accustomed to competency-based progress, don't want to wait.

"They turned out exactly as we intended," she says. "We create the currency and then get angry that they're dealing in our currency. We say being an officer is a big deal and you see the perks that go with that, then when they say 'I want some of that,' we slap their hands. It's the grown-up version of the trophies we gave them when they were playing soccer. We taught them that work ethic. We bring them into the corporate settings where we say the corner office is important or the title is important. If we were to ask them rather than tell them, if we allowed them to shape their currency, we could leverage their capabilities much more successfully.

"These are the kids who grew up with video games. They knew video games from the time they could hold a controller in their hands. What video games have taught them is when you complete a level, you get the next level, and when you complete that level it entitles you to the next level. Then they come into the workforce, and you say, 'Here are the requirements.' Why put in time until you reach the next level? Clearly, I'm ready for the next level. I met all the requirements."

Successful companies will learn to take the Millennials' experience and desires into account. Rather than "work-life balance," a tricky juggling of competing claims, they expect a flexible, person-directed, life that integrates the range of relationships and activities.

Howe saw a dramatic shift in military recruiting as the first Millennials arrived at recruiting stations around 2000.

> *These thirty-year gunnery sergeants were saying, 'We don't understand these kids today,'" he recalls. "'They're coming into the recruiting depots and bringing their moms with them.' This recruiter is completely dumbfounded. If you understand who Millennials are, you would understand why they would do that. Millennials want to fit in, do what's expected and help members of the team. Army ads now show moms and dads and feature large groups of people doing things in unison, usually good things for the world.*

The relationship focus organizes all of life for many Millennials. For one thing, Howe says, they relate freely with their parents, a far cry from the 1960s slogan: "Never trust anyone over thirty."

> *They listen to the same songs, watch the same movies, and wear the same brand of clothing. This is amazing. You have Millennials playing Rock Band or Guitar Hero or learning to do Led Zeppelin riffs at their summer camp. Back when Boomers were that age, there was not one artifact of our parents' that we would touch. Parents expected the same resentment and didn't get it. This is an amazing shift.*

In 2013, a record 36 percent of people eighteen to thirty-one years old were living with their parents—up from 32 percent in 2007. That included 16 percent of those twenty-five to thirty-one years old, along with 56 percent of those eighteen to twenty-four, the typical college years when students list their parents' residence, and 18 percent of those with at least a bachelor's degree. For some, that reflects an insistence on leading a seamless life, including work.

Some observers characterize Millennials as risk-averse, on subjects from stock market investments to illegal behavior. For example, the arrest rate for juveniles ages ten to eighteen in 2010 plummeted by more than 35 percent from 1994, and prison populations are down, especially among younger people, for a variety of reasons. Millennials are not investing in risky stocks for retirement as Boomers and Xers have done, partly because they saw the devastation of their parents' accounts in 2008. Instead, they are more frugal with their money, paying bills, saving cash, and avoiding excessive debt, partly because many already carry much student debt. In that way they resemble earlier generations, with Boomers' and Xers' retirement obsession as the outlier historically.

Millennials are more focused on life now rather than decades away, with more saving for vacations or travel rather than retirement, and they insist on a seamless life, including work.

"They don't even know there is an eight to five," Barnhart says. "They don't have that paradigm to work from. We heard a lot of 'I want meaningful work. I want the flexibility to design how and when I'm going to do the work. Engage me in a way that allows me to feel successful.' I think they're just expressing their human needs more out ahead of other things. If they don't define themselves by title or position, it inherently gives them greater freedom. They don't define themselves in that way. It gives them a completely different lens. They see the possibility of starting their own businesses. The possibilities are much greater now than they were when I was their age. You couldn't do an Internet start-up kind of thing. Maybe some of it is we just have this sort of secret envy of that generation. In some ways they're striving differently for some of the same things that baby boomers imagined but never quite achieved. I could look at it through the lens of this as the generation that possibly could change everything."

CONCLUSION

As promised, this discussion has not provided a key, formula, or secret to understanding the Millennials you encounter. Its aim was to show you why there is no such thing. Your best chance is to understand the environment where these people have grown up, to resist the categorizing temptation, and to engage the person in front of you as an individual with the unique mindset, skills, perspectives, and passions that such an environment has empowered.

That would be a fruitful way to relate to any person of any generation. Any other approach runs the risk, at least, of stereotyping, prejudice, and misunderstanding. "Never trust anyone over thirty" is as unhelpful as "What's the matter with kids these days?" The temptation to classify is understandably strong. Getting to "know" a group, to assume a set of characteristics, saves the multiplied work of getting to know each individual in that group. It's easier to say "All soldiers are heroes" and discount bad-apple atrocities like Abu Ghraib, or to say "All CEOs are rapacious" and discount the good works of Bill Gates and Warren Buffett, than to treat each soldier or CEO as an individual person. And there are, in fact, cultures that provide identities, accepted by their members in general, that should be respected by outsiders. It's not biased stereotyping to offer gifts to an Asian business partner or understand the personal-space expectations of friends from other cultures.

But the presumptions of the past were based largely on formal structures broadly accepted—from correct business attire and the sequence of dinner silverware to, in some cases, the proper role of women and minorities in corporate and social settings. Those structures are no longer so broadly accepted. Instead, the commonly observed informality of Millennials apparently reflects a rejection, explicit or not, of singular, static ideal forms in favor of multiple-choice, dynamic diversity. The resistance to tie-and-jacket office uniforms may have the same source as the resistance to the eight-hour workday clock and the years of dues-paying for an already-qualified worker.

Even then, the embrace of diversity leaves open the past forms as a possible choice. As in cyberspace, nothing really disappears, and eclectic freedom can select the old-fashioned, the revolutionary, something between, or an idiosyncratic combination. You cannot know in the case of a particular person without making the effort to find out. And learning one fact does not confirm presumably related assumptions—Millennials' overwhelming support for gay marriage, for example, does not come with a corresponding support for abortion, where they may be more "conservative" than their parents. The labels do not hold.

If you are not a Millennial, it's important to remember: Each generation, past, present, and future, grows up with unique experiences that yield different perspectives, each worthy of respect. Try to understand them not in terms of your experience, but in terms of theirs—which this book has attempted to convey. The calendar years of Millennials, their laps around the Sun, have been filled with more stimulation, more information, and more connection than you would have at a similar stage of your life. They are even experiencing puberty earlier—between 1997 and 2013, the percent of girls who start to develop breasts by age seven has jumped from 5 percent to 10 percent for white girls and 15 percent to 23 percent for black girls. Meanwhile, they are watching less television. In 2014 they watched an average of 20.5 hours a week, at least half of the time their parents spent—although the decrease may result partly from their access to some of the same programming through subscription video-on-demand services like Netflix or Hulu. By 2014, 40 percent of American households had subscriptions.

In addition, they are also spending more time online, where the experience is far more interactive and collaborative. In particular, they spend more time using social media than following news, and when they do check the news, it's more likely to be from digital sources than traditional media. Argument-settling facts that not so long ago required a trip to the library are at their fingertips. Where you scheduled a call to Mom when long-distances rates were most favorable, they call across the world for free through smartphones or Skype. These capacities are not their exclusive property—they are in principle available to people of every age—but they are uniquely their lifelong experience and their reflexive mental habits. The world is moving so fast for Millennials, with one technology rapidly superseding another throughout their lives, that twenty-somethings have already developed nostalgia for the video games they played in grade school—and companies are responding strongly to this market by rereleasing updated versions of such "classics." Millennials are even driving a revival of vinyl records, a technology that hardly any of them could remember well from their own younger-days experience. This revival has increased vinyl sales by more than 900 percent since 2005!

An old story from India about blind men and an elephant warns against assuming that the whole can be inferred from the parts. In the English poetic version by John Godfrey Saxe, the six men variously mistake the side for a wall, the tusk for a spear, the trunk for a snake, the leg for a tree, the ear for a fan, and the tail for a rope. Any attempt to talk about the Millennial generation runs at least the same risk of mistakes, and more. An encounter with a member of this generation is not an encounter with the generation as a whole, or a prediction of what the next encounter will involve. Beyond that, the individuals in this generation are whole persons, not parts of something else where they find their proper meaning, identity, and function. There is no elephant in the room.

Your best chance of understanding the Millennial in front of you is not as a "Millennial" but as the person in front of you. That, of course, would also be preferable for everyone you meet, as many of the Millennials already know. Out of that background, Millennials have grown to be impatient when it comes to organizations, hierarchies, or even public policies that bend toward exclusion rather than inclusion. In the case of Abercrombie & Fitch, heavily influenced by tendencies reminiscent of the Silent Generation, when Millennials experienced their liberties being compromised and saw mistreatment of their friends, they acted.

Chapter 7

THE CHANGE:
Deliberately Disruptive Diversity Dialogues

The milestone passed quietly, maybe noticed first deep in the human resources department or General Counsel's Office of Abercrombie & Fitch: for the first time, in the companies more than one hundred eighteen-year history, more than half of the brand's one hundred thousand store associates were nonwhite. By 2011, that was hardly news—the upward trend had been clear for years, just as the trend is clear that the United States will become a majority-minority country by 2043. Abercrombie & Fitch was just ahead of the curve. And its customers were as diverse as its workforce. In 2011, as in 2009, an independent marketing firm found that the Hollister brand ranked number one among African American youth ages eight to fifteen.

For me, the numbers were a promise kept—I set the new trajectory when I arrived in 2004 as Chief Diversity Officer, overseeing a key part of the settlement of the Millennials' lawsuit. We created an Executive Diversity Council in 2006, sponsored hundreds of multicultural events and minority-focused recruiting efforts, launched a scholarship program with the National Society of High School Scholars, inaugurated Diversity Week and a Diversity Champion Program, established diversity councils in stores and distribution centers, and exported diversity awareness as the company expanded around the globe.

The little-traveled road to corporate diversity was long,

sometimes rocky, and, like Fitch Path, more winding than straight. Embarrassing bumps, spinouts, and crashes—individual or institutional, unfair or self-inflicted, damaging or rallying—had impeded the progress and threatened the journey. This marker was more proof that the company was moving in the right direction.

WASP OUTFITTER'S FIRST CENTURY

The rise of the Millennial generation's culture, tastes, and preferences—and their desirable and diverse market—has caught many organizations off guard. Older corporate leaders who thought they could maintain profit by repeating the process that the U.S. market had always favored quickly found themselves irrelevant and left behind. Companies must both understand the past and chart a new course into the future, setting a tone at the very top—independent directors and C-Suite executives—that embraces the realities of the twenty-first century. When I came to Abercrombie, I became part of an organization that had experienced considerable success with older business models for decades.

Founded in New York in the Gilded Age by David Abercrombie, soon partnered with Ezra Fitch, the store catered to wealthy, WASP-y sportsmen and outfitted safaris from Teddy Roosevelt to Ernest Hemingway. Charles Lindbergh wore an Abercrombie outfit for his pioneering New York-to-Paris solo flight in 1927, and Amelia Earhart donned an Abercrombie six-button suede jacket for her own transatlantic trip alone five years later. John Kennedy picked out his blazers and shirts for weekend relaxing at the store, around the same time that John Steinbeck reported his own shopping there in *Travels with Charley: In Search of America*. Steinbeck wrote:

> *Some years ago at Abercrombie & Fitch, I bought a cattle caller, an automatic horn manipulated by a lever with which nearly all cow emotions can be imitated, from the sweet lowing of a romantic heifer to the growling roar of a bull in the prime*

and lust of his bullhood.... I showed him some fancy jigs and
poppers I'd bought at Abercrombie and Fitch, and gave him
one, and I gave him some paperback thrillers I'd finished with,
all loaded with sex and sadism, and also a copy of Field and
Stream.

Abercrombie & Fitch was ahead of its time in marketing—
spending heavily on a 456-page 1909 catalogue, with advice columns
and articles as well as camping gear and outdoor clothing advertise-
ments, that it mailed to more than fifty thousand people. The next year,
the store broke tradition by selling to women as well as men. During the
Roaring Twenties, "The Greatest Sporting Goods Store in the World"
filled a twelve-story building on Madison Avenue, with different floors
for clothing, games, fishing, guns, and a shooting gallery.

Abercrombie & Fitch was also a social trendsetter—the store
sold hip flasks during Prohibition and was the first importer of Mahjong
games from China in 1920, selling more than twelve thousand sets.
Sales fell from $6.3 million in 1929 to $2.6 million in 1933 because
of the Great Depression but rebounded by 1938, when gun sales
contributed heavily along with clothing, shoes, and accessories.

"The Abercrombie & Fitch type does not care about the cost;
he wants the finest quality," President Otis Guernsey bragged in the
1950s, when the store was opening new upscale locations across
the country, including San Francisco, and seasonal shops in places
like Palm Beach and Sarasota, Florida; Bayhead, New Jersey; and
Southampton, New York. In the 1964 comedy *Man's Favorite Sport?*,
Rock Hudson starred as a salesman for Abercrombie & Fitch, Roger
Willoughby, who pretended to be a fishing expert and was blackmailed
by PR executive Abigail Page, played by Paula Prentiss, into a fishing
tournament that revealed his haplessness.

New stores opened in upscale locations through the 1960s—
Colorado Springs in 1962, The Mall at Short Hills in New Jersey in
1963, Bal Harbour Shops near Miami Beach in 1966, Somerset Mall
in suburban Detroit in 1969. But sales and profits slid in the late 1960s
and early 1970s, when quirky ads, including the first TV commercial in

Figure 1: The inner cover of Abercrombie and Fitch Co.'s first catalog, 1909.

1969, and massive sales promotions backfired by attracting customers "not of classic Abercrombie & Fitch material," according to President William Humphreys. The company lost $1 million in 1976, filed for bankruptcy, and closed in 1977.

The next year, Oshman Sporting Goods bought the Abercrombie & Fitch name and attempted to revive the brand, even reprising the outfitting of celebrities—Jack Lemmon to fish in Alaska and Steve Garvey to hunt grouse in Minnesota. In the next decade, Oshman opened twenty-seven stores from Beverly Hills to New York, with some flashy echoes of the old days—a convertible sports car called the Abercrombie Runabout, $40,000 elephant guns—but mostly modern sports equipment such as exercise machines and tennis rackets, along with gifts and clothing.

Limited Brands paid $47 million for twenty-five of the stores in 1988 and increased the focus on menswear, followed by women's clothing and gifts. Michael Jeffries became president in 1992 and launched a transformation to high-end clothes for the growing young-adult market—a self-proclaimed aim for the brand to "sizzle with sex." With this in mind, Jeffries hired Bruce Weber—famed for, among other things, his photographs of Tom Hintnaus and Marcus Schenkenberg in Calvin Klein ads—to produce images for the catalog and advertising. Sales soared to $85 million in 1992, $111 million in 1993, and $165 million in 1994.

Beginning in 1997, the company published the A&F Quarterly, a "magalog"—part lifestyle magazine, part catalog—with little or no clothing on the cavorting models in the front and no people wearing the outfits advertised in the back. The publication reached a circulation of 1.2 million, including two hundred thousand sold in stores. The sexually intensive marketing—an updated version of the ground-breaking 1909 catalog with a modern twist on Steinbeck's "sweet lowing of a romantic heifer to the growling roar of a bull in the prime and lust of his bullhood"—provoked outrage from older generations. In 1998, Mothers Against Drunk Driving protested a Back-to-School Quarterly that included cocktail recipes in its Drinking 101 section, and a "who's who" of religious organizations—the National Coalition for the Protection of Children and Families, the American Decency Association, Focus on the Family—railed against what they saw as its soft-porn images and promotion of college sex. The National Organization for Women and some state elected officials joined the protest when images appeared to promote violent and potentially illegal activity. Such controversy, contrary to their mission, was usually so much free publicity to the company whose strategy involved spending no money on marketing outside of the look and feel of its stores and their Brand Representatives.

Smaller Abercrombie & Fitch stores in high-traffic areas proliferated, and sales reached $805.2 million in 1998. Sales topped $1 billion the next year, when Limited spun off Abercrombie & Fitch's more than two hundred stores and it went public as ANF, for sixteen dollars a share, on the New York Stock Exchange. In 2000, the company launched its Hollister brand, a West Coast style named for a stretch of California beach popular with surfers, that complemented its East Coast tradition and aimed for a high school demographic slightly younger than its collegiate core. Ruehl No. 925, a store that targeted young professionals among their twenties and thirties and whose image consisted of college graduates aspiring to New York City style success, started in 2004, and Gilly Hicks, an Australian "Down Under" themed underwear specialty store, opened in 2008. Sluggish sales during the national recession and Abercrombie & Fitch's increasing focus on international expansion led it to close Ruehl. In 2013, the company announced that it would close freestanding Gilly Hicks stores the next year and planned to market the products through Hollister and online.

In the summer of 1999, the male pop trio LFO (Lyte Funky Ones), released "Summer Girls," the lead single on their album, which had two oft-repeated lines about ANF: "I like girls that wear Abercrombie & Fitch. I'd take her if I had one wish" and "When I met you, I said my name is Rich. You look like a girl from Abercrombie & Fitch." The performance was a one-hit wonder for LFO, whose mass appeal quickly faded.

Chapter 8

MY ROLE AT ABERCROMBIE

I joined the company during a period of rapid expansion, with opportunities to innovate and instigate change in ways that directly impacted public image. I was older than the Millennials that I was managing, and the iGens who came to work before I left, but the office on Fitch Path was heavy on Xer's and Baby Boomers, and the CEO was from the Silent Generation. As I oriented myself to the culture, I consciously and regularly noted after each interaction with a peer and other senior leaders where they were on their own personal diversity journeys. I grouped them into three categories:

1. The Struggler, an individual who finds it difficult to rally around the need for change, see the value in a diversity initiative, or embrace the necessary behavioral changes.

2. The Neutral Observer, an individual who is on the fence about the initiative—they won't actively resist, but they will be passive-aggressive about what should be done and how.

3. The Diversity Champion, a person whose curiosity about different personal attributes is reinforced by their courage to challenge inappropriate responses to those differences, even if there is some personal risk to their own future professional success.

This insight is crucial for any diversity effort because it identifies people you can count on when you need to nudge someone and hold them accountable. It also allows you to gauge your workplace environment and stay alert to those who might create a distraction during the implementation phase.

Even though I'm an Xer, I represented the company everywhere I went. In 2011, I wore my Abercrombie jeans, oxford shirt, and cardigan sweater to the Working Mother Media's Multicultural Women's National Conference at a hotel in Times Square where everyone else was wearing suits. Pamela Babcock, a writer for the Society for Human Resource Management, was there and asked about the outfit. "If I go to an event where I'm representing A&F, I can't wear a suit," I told her. "I'm sure it would raise eyebrows and the question, 'Is that what you sell?' We all wear our products, every day."

I grew up in Long Island, New York, and my career started on a much more boring track. My summer internships at Carrier, a United Technologies company, landed me a job in the firm's financial planning group after I earned a degree in finance from LeMoyne College in Syracuse, New York, in 1991. The internships were arranged by INROADS, an international organization founded in Chicago in 1970 and aimed at boosting talented minority students' exposure to the corporate world. After four years at Carrier, still thinking about my mentoring and developmental experiences with INROADS, I decided to aim for more people-oriented work. I started to figure out that there might be something else I could get into—helping people integrate and be part of a culture that doesn't look like them. Back then, they didn't call it diversity. They were reaching out to the community to bring in people who looked different. That was a pretty significant step in my life.

I left Carrier and went to Georgetown University to earn an MBA concentrating on organizational development and change management, where my career path was confirmed. It clicked that there was something I could do for a living that focused on diversity and inclusion. I spent six years as a senior consultant and New York office leader at Towers Perrin's, now Towers Watson, Global Diversity and Change Management Practice in Manhattan, with clients from aerospace to utilities and a heavy load from the consumer products, financial services, and pharmaceuticals industries. Issues varied from threatening nooses in factory lockers to women on Wall Street who quit because of men's "boyish" behavior.

It was common to see white male executives in places like the New York Stock Exchange or PaineWebber, now UBS, feel ill-equipped to comprehend the problems, define the business case for diversity, and develop any sense of urgency around creating a diversity strategy.

The issues I saw made me realize diversity and inclusion are more complicated than I thought. There was a big gap between what people know and what I took for granted. For a lot of them, they got it because they realized they had a daughter or son-in-law who was experiencing something they had never experienced themselves. They figured out they had something to learn from me.

After six years of consulting, I decided to find work where I could oversee larger projects from start to finish. I went to Starwood Hotels & Resorts Worldwide as senior manager of diversity for two years before Abercrombie called with the chance to build a program from the ground up, reporting directly to the Chairman and CEO, Michael S. Jeffries.

OFFICE OF DIVERSITY: PROFIT INCLUDED

In 2012, Abercrombie & Fitch won its seventh "Best Place to work for LGBT Equality" honor from the Human Rights Campaign. The tide had turned in the United States on the subject of equality, diversity, and inclusion, as the nation's Millennial population presaged profound shifts in attitudes and demographics, and the onetime WASPish Abercrombie & Fitch was ahead of the curve. The store already had a majority-minority staff, store associates participated in a rainbow of inclusion-promoting activities, and because of my role in the success, many businesses were calling for advice as they recognized the economic value of mirroring the face of the market. They wanted to hear not only the creative ways we engaged Millennials at work around "purpose, passion, and productivity" but how I personally recycled the energy and vulnerability of youthful exuberance that was in ample supply across the stores' associate population, all the while displaying organizational maturity and managerial courage as we pushed through internal headwinds and crosswinds.

Within a year after I moved into the office on Fitch Path, I had installed a Diversity & Inclusion portal on the company website. The consent decree that created the Office of Diversity came with an unusually detailed set of benchmarks for progress in diversifying the workforce of a company that was ranked by Piper Jaffray's shopping survey—for the sixth consecutive year—as the number one teen brand in the United States. Translation: I had a unique opportunity to be imaginative, think beyond the box, and draw outside of the lines in order to stay in front of the "race toward diversity."

We established a Diversity & Inclusion team and hired more than two dozen diversity recruiters, exceeding the decree's requirements, and created an Executive Diversity Council. Abercrombie & Fitch gave $300,000 of scholarship money to the United Negro College Fund and launched other minority-focused recruitment efforts. I crisscrossed the country personally visiting historically black colleges and universities (HBCUs) and schools on the West Coast with a high percentage of Asian American college students, to hear from them directly about what a successfully implemented diversity initiative would look like; they would measure our success.

African Americans, Latinos, and Asian Americans, who had accounted for 9 percent of the workforce when the Gonzalez lawsuit was filed and inched to 10.63 percent while the settlement was under negotiation, soared to 20.64 percent by April 2006.

"This is a very important case to the EEOC," explained Greg Gochanour, of the federal agency's San Francisco office. "It's a case of significant public interest, and the ability to turn things around at this company, in this case, I think will send, if it works out, a very good message in terms of the enforcement of Title VII."

When leaders from both sides of the lawsuit gathered with Judge Susan Illston for the first annual status reports on August 22, 2006, monitor Fred Alvarez praised the early efforts.

"I can say I got a hundred percent cooperation from all the parties, and they did everything they could to make my job easier," said Alvarez, who had met with the leaders three times. "The parties were very collaborative."

Alvarez had traveled to Fitch Path to interview the Chief Executive Officer, the Chief Operating Officer, and the head of human resources, as well as meeting several times with me. He had also interviewed more than one hundred employees and some twenty people who had used the newly implemented complaint process. He had visited twenty-five stores across the country and conducted a formal audit of seventeen of them.

"I developed a protocol for how to go into a store and interview employees, managers, how to interview the diversity of recruiters, borrowed on my experience at the government, both at the National Labor Relations Board and the EEOC and at the Department of Labor," Alvarez told the court. He also reviewed two thick six-month progress reports, produced by the company, and me, to prepare for the meeting.

"I concluded that the [Diversity] office was adequately funded," Alvarez said. "I concluded that it was highly visible in the organization, that Mr. Corley had access to the highest levels and to his own colleagues. I concluded that Mr. Corley is a very qualified person for the job—and I may not have fit it in the report, but I'll say it here—I think he brings vision and energy to the position that he has, and is realistic about the challenges that he has, but he has some more challenges to overcome. But I think Abercrombie has done an excellent job in selecting him and establishing this office. The office has a lot of responsibilities, and I think Mr. Corley has done a good job of leveraging his own resources to try to get some of those things done…. Bottom line, the Office of Diversity, I think, was a successful implementation."

Abercrombie & Fitch, as directed by the decree, had hired Kathleen Lundquist, a professional industrial organizational psychologist, to develop a written job analysis and job-related criteria for each in-store position. In the first six months, the company exceeded the decree's minority hiring requirements. Although it missed most of the higher goals in the second six months, the plaintiffs took an approach of vigilant patience as systems matured across the six-year settlement period. Alvarez pointed out that some new managers had missed diversity training because of the company's high turnover rate, and some interviewers had not implemented the new job description requirements effectively. "It can be a very subjective judgment, and if they don't have proper guidance and some notion of who's more qualified than somebody else, there's a potential for adverse impact," he said. "I guess I'd conclude by saying I think everybody here is trying to make this successful. I was pleased, as I said, with the cooperation of both sides."

Abercrombie & Fitch representative Mark Knueve said the company had developed an electronic application kiosk that allowed job-seekers to submit applications electronically and enabled the company to track application and hire statistics. "Over the course of the past year, the company more than doubled, and in some cases tripled, the incumbency of African Americans, Asian Americans and Latinos in the company's part-time in-store population and full-time managerial population," he said. "Abercrombie has a plan in place to achieve the hiring benchmarks."

Bill Lann Lee, the plaintiffs' lead attorney, pointed out that the missed benchmarks translated into some four thousand jobs across the company. He insisted that Abercrombie & Fitch should boost the diversity of its marketing materials—perhaps also creating an "image book" to show managers what was meant by diversity—to improve the hiring rates. "It's to Abercrombie's credit that they agreed to and then have set forth in a very good-hearted way to implement what the Court herself characterized as a very detailed, comprehensive decree," Lee said. "This is a document that has required of Abercrombie substantial work, substantial commitment of resources, and I think everyone on the plaintiffs' side of the table thinks that it is to their credit that they have done in many ways an exceptional job."

Company representative Thomas Ridgley, who welcomed the idea of an image book, explained that "marketing" was different for Abercrombie & Fitch than for other retailers. "Abercrombie is unique in respect of the fact that it does not do advertising on television or radio, doesn't do Gap or Old Navy–type advertising—the in-store experience is the entire advertising experience," he said.

Abercrombie & Fitch won its first "Best Place to work for LGBT Equality" recognition in 2006, and the efforts accelerated through the court-supervised six years and beyond. In 2007, the company sponsored more than twenty multicultural events, and by the next year more than one-third of its Brand Representatives were people of color. In 2008, Abercrombie & Fitch launched a scholarship program with the National Society of High School Scholars, chaired by Claes Nobel, patriarch of the prize-founding family, aimed at promoting success through diversity for teens and tweens.

Abercrombie & Fitch attracted unexpected attention in the spring of 2008 when three young men, all wearing different A&F t-shirts, appeared behind presidential candidate Barack Obama at an April 22 speech in Evansville, Indiana. One of the men worked at the company's Evansville store, and he and his brother, with another friend, happened to wear their t-shirts to the rally, where campaign officials asked them to take the camera-friendly seats. The event sparked a mini-media frenzy, from CNN to the *New York Times*, about the Abercrombie Boys, speculating that the brand was seeking strategic exposure to the same young people energized by Obama's candidacy. The men, who would not let reporters use their names, said their choice of t-shirts was mere coincidence and they had not expected to make news.

By that year, 35 percent of the company's eighty-eight thousand in-store workers were nonwhite. As a firm believer in measuring change, I urged "secret shoppers" to self-identify in a new program where they tested stores to make sure minorities received the same treatment as whites—how many items allowed in the dressing room or whether or not you were greeted in the first fifteen seconds of entering the store, for example. A monthly list identified the top twenty-five and bottom twenty-five for diversity hiring. The Santa Monica store where Juancarlos Gomez-Montejano was fired nine years earlier won the 2008 award for greatest staff diversity, chosen by my team from photographs submitted by each store. The winning picture was a multihued gathering of Brand Representatives—the satirical MADtv tableau transformed into a real-life model of diversity that reflected the company's in-store staff.

I had established a committee to weigh the views and concerns of the Millennial generation with its new understanding of diversity. "We're talking about young people who have different ideas about what diversity means," I told *Racing Toward Diversity* magazine in 2012. "They want to be with everybody, not the 'black group' or the 'Hispanic group.'" We hired professional actors for an interactive theater with district managers, based on interviews to gather store associates' perspectives, to boost awareness of diversity and inclusion. The power of interactive theater is priceless. It's a technique that allows you to tap into the emotional and real-time reaction to the most common or complicated workplace issues, while "watching" the situation unfold in front of your eyes. The learning is significant for today's generation because it allows them as participants to see, hear, and respond to the teachable moments as opposed to relying on just reading something in a textbook and hoping that it sticks. What better way for a generation that grew up on gaming and connecting with people directly to change behavior, find the right way to give employee feedback as a new manager, or have courageous conversations around disciplinary issues?

ERASING EXCLUSION

In 2009, my office launched a Diversity Week and a Diversity Champion program, and we devised an "If you really knew me" activity based on an MTV reality show. In this adaptation, participants pick three different diversity variables from a customized Inclusion Wheel to describe themselves at management meetings. The wheel places a Personality layer at the heart of four concentric circles: an Internal layer including physical/mental ability, race, age, gender, ethnicity, sexual orientation, and national origin; an External layer including family,

Figure 2: An inclusion wheel template.

parental status, relationship/marital status, appearance, geographic location, work experience, citizenship, belief system/religion, socioeconomic status, educational background, hobbies/individual interests, and personal experience; an Organizational layer including work location, job title, time with company, brand, and department; and an Era layer, including cultural events, political events, world events, and generational events. We made a week-long activity about it. We did a lot of interactive things to make it fun, including scenario-based learning with alternative endings for a diversity champion, one who struggles with diversity, and a neutral observer.

Associates used the wheel to get to know each other, especially during Diversity & Inclusion Week with its #EraseExclusion emphasis. "Select a dimension you've become more open about," one activity suggested. "Who or what experience inspired you to be more open about that dimension?" In the Inclusion Challenge, they were encouraged to submit music videos or original songs up to two minutes; original photographs, paintings, drawings, or collages with explanatory paragraphs; and poems or essays up to three hundred words. Winning stores and individuals received prizes and recognition on the A&F United Facebook page. Inclusion Challenge submissions provided Abercrombie & Fitch associates an opportunity to share experiences of their own and to better understand the experiences of others. The submissions revealed the breadth of diversity among the individuals that make up the company.

The submissions, which were published and distributed at multicultural events, made available to the general public online, and shared across key strategic diversity partners secured by my team, offered a glance into what I uncovered about the personal journeys associates were traveling. These are among my favorites in the public domain.

From Kelli:

> *I have always been a passionate advocate for inclusion, but it wasn't until my own sense of comfort was tested that I came to understand the full scope of the word. I was an Overnight Manager at a Hollister in 2006 and had worked hard to create an inclusive atmosphere in my store. Everyone found it easy to get along and work well together because they all came from the same area and had similar backgrounds. When my GM told me that he would be hiring a new overnighter that was deaf, I was concerned about the way the other members of my overnight team would respond to her. I struggled to give Lynn an orientation and found communicating to be extremely difficult. I soon realized that I was the one who needed to step up and make a change to ensure that she did not feel different when she came to our store.*
>
> *Before her first shift, I spent a few weeks learning as much sign language as I could. I knew she would not be able to communicate on my level, and so I had to communicate on hers. I taught myself to sign the alphabet and learn the words "size stickers," "shelf," "flip-flops," "shirts," and "jeans." After that, I taught myself to sign all of the colors and sizes and learned to say "rebuild the wall." I was nervous at first, but after several hours of pointing and using my hands to communicate the best that I could, she completed her first update presentation. Many of my overnighters came to me and said that they didn't think she would ever fit in and that they were frustrated that she took so long to complete her presentations. I challenged them back and said that they were the ones that needed to make a change in order to communicate with her. I could tell by her dedication and enthusiasm that she would soon be one of our most valuable employees. I taught all of my overnighters to sign the alphabet and paired one of them with her during each shift. I told them that they were required to get to know her and had to let me know at the end of their*

shifts what they had learned about her personality. After a few weeks, Lynn was truly beginning to fit in with the team and everyone was excited to see her when she would come in for her shift.

Lynn felt so comfortable in her new workplace that she told some of her friends who were also deaf about the job. Many of them interviewed well and were added to our team. Because they were able to communicate with the other overnighters, they had no problem adjusting to the new job. I taught them how to build closets, audit, and standardize all through signing. After a few months, we had nine people on our team who were deaf, and that summer, I completed my first floor set with no words. Because they could not hear, their ability to notice small details was enhanced. I passed out all of the documents, pointed to the details and location on the map, and let them go. They executed their presentations flawlessly. It was one of the most successful floor sets I have ever been a part of. A few years later, Lynn sent me an email and thanked me for helping her become a part of our team. She said it was the first job that she had where she did not feel different. For myself, I learned that sometimes I need to challenge my own preconceived ideas of what will "work." I learned that all it takes to make an associate successful is an environment in which they feel valued and giving them the knowledge and skills they need to thrive. I learned that everyone is teachable, even myself!

From Karla:

As a Part-Time Impact associate working in Abercrombie Kids located in downtown San Francisco for almost one year, I have noticed that most of our customers are tourists, mostly Europeans. Whenever I have the chance to go on the sales floor to run items or do a task on the sales floor, from far away I can hear the tourists talking in their native languages over the phone or to their children. However, the situation that made me think about Erasing Exclusion was the first time I heard a customer talking in a language familiar to me—Spanish. My first language is Spanish, and knowing that there was a Spanish-speaking customer in the store made me happy and eager to help her and her two daughters.

Thousands of thoughts began running through my head in just seconds. "Should I use the taglines in English or translate them in Spanish? What if I speak to them in English and they get mad because they can tell I speak Spanish?" I ignored the thoughts, approached the customer and her daughters, and said to them with a smile, "Hey! How's it going? Habla Español?" After they looked at me surprised and then gave me a smile, the mother responded to me in Spanish how great it was that I could speak Spanish, and I helped her daughters to a fitting room, verified the price of the clearance items she had, and even helped her pick some clothes for her thirteen-year-old son who had asked her to buy him some specific clothes!

When they finished trying on the clothes and picking out clothes for her son, the woman told me she was ready to pay if I could help her. I told her I do not do cash registers, but I took her to the cash registers so she could be helped. She thanked me a lot for helping her because she said she thought it was impossible to have a Spanish-speaking associate in Abercrombie. I told her not to worry about it, that it was my pleasure to help her, and to have a safe trip back to Spain. I walked back to the stockroom thinking about how great it was using my Spanish-speaking skills and hoping that I can encounter more situations like this so I can provide great customer service skills. I believe that it would be great if all the associates can use their languages other than English to help customers whenever they have a chance, because they will greatly appreciate it and have a great, comfortable shopping experience.

From Sarah:

#Erase Exclusion

Looking through another's eyes
Will give you strength and make you wise.

There's always more than what you see,
To understand is to be free…

…Free to make a better choice
To heal a life, to hear a voice.

…Free to be a guiding light
To take the wrongs and make them right!

Close your eyes and open your heart;
The ripples of change must somehow start.

Don't whisper, gossip, judge or chide.
Include, invite, help change the tide.

The world belongs to all of us!
Fill it with friendship, love and trust.

From Sabrina:

Fifty years ago on the steps of the Lincoln Memorial, Dr. Martin Luther King gave a speech that changed American history, encouraging people of every creed to join in the front for equality. Though the speech promoted the growth of the Civil Rights Movement, not all of the problems are gone today. As society grows and values evolve, what once was a problem of yesterday becomes obsolete, but still history has a way of repeating itself. Though the format of the problem has changed, its essence remains the same. Exclusion remains at the root of all problems. In my particular case, it wasn't a case of prejudice or racism, it was just a matter of fitting in.

Like every good Asian, I was taught to associate with my own kind, but did my own kind accept me? All throughout school (elementary from high school) I never seemed to fit in or "click" with other Asians. No matter how hard I tried, my attempts were met with, at best, lukewarm affection. Having tried hanging out with "cool" Asians, "nerdy" Asians, and "Asian" Asians, I was beginning to feel like a girl dumped before prom. "Is it me?" I wondered. Am I not smart/pretty/cool enough? I was never invited to their swim parties, never in the cool gaggle of kids at my lunch table (I always sat at the edge by the garbage cans). Then the answer to my problems became clear: I was looking in the wrong place. I realized that hanging out with Asians wasn't a necessity. Surely I wasn't going to bring dishonor upon my family for being friends with people outside my own race.

Slowly but surely I started talking to people outside of math club and Chinese club. I started attending theater meetings. I opened my eyes to a whole new life outside of Asians. I said good-bye to my old "friends" (they weren't all that upset) and hello to new ones. I learned that I was funny (none of my Asian friends ever laughed at my jokes). For the first time in my adolescent life, I felt like I belonged. I had finally found my niche. I am now the Secretary of Troupe 3689, our school's theater troupe, and proud to say that I am friends with people of multiple races, religions, and sexualities, just like Dr. King would have wanted.

From Bess:

Race to Erase

Every day is a step toward new change.
Reverse the old steps and open up to a broad range.
As we work together we can erase the past.
Surely our motivation can create an inclusive future that will last.
Explore the differences that are unique to each special kind and
Eventually this will open us up to a different set of mind.
X out the word discrimination,
Cause we are now in an inclusive generation.
Love, accept, and give everyone a chance.
Undo the past and show the world our new stance.
So now let's work together to do what's right.
Include everyone and the world will slowly shine bright.
On the count of three, we will erase exclusion and discrimination.
Now we can be the world's new inspiration.

The D&I office started Diversity Councils in stores and distribution centers in 2010. That year, DiversityExecutive.com published a feature article with me, "From bland to brand." "When you are challenged by somebody on the outside looking in or people internally wondering what you're all about, you can point to, 'Here are the things we've done in this space' — if it's the LGBT community, the African-American community, whatever it is; your diversity brand is essentially tied to: What have you really done?" I told the publication. "There's a correlation between the diversity of our associates and the reputation we've embraced because people are applying; they're being hired in different positions that cross the spectrum of roles and responsibilities; and I would argue because of that, people who see them say, 'I can be there, too.'"

Minorities had already reached 49 percent of all the Brand Representatives when I gave the interview, and we crossed the 50 percent milestone the following year. Abercrombie & Fitch had expanded to Canada in 2005 and opened its first European store in London in 2007. The first store in Paris had opened by 2011 with one hundred shirtless male models lined up in front of the thirty-one-thousand-square-foot store on the historical Champs-Elysees—until police forced them to cover up because of a law banning partial nudity on the street. The same year, Abercrombie & Fitch became a sponsor of the European Diversity Awards, and diversity training for international managers started the year after.

As a person on the list of Top 100 Executives in such magazines as *Uptown Professional* and *Savoy*, I was a keynote panelist for the Linkage Diversity Conference in Atlanta and for the U.S. Department of State's Diversity Thought Leaders Conference in Washington, D.C., in 2012. I was interviewed in *Forbes* magazine for the article "Diversity must become a profit center for enterprise to flourish" ahead of the Linkage conference.

"At A&F, we focus on three areas to drive [diversity] ROI. First, in-store experience," I told the magazine. "We want to make our customer feel excited about what happens when you walk into the store. Whether you are Latino or Asian we want them all to connect with our brand and feel the experience. Second, employee engagement—we want our employees to see people that look like them and/or people they would like to 'hang out' with. Finally, we believe in driving 'diversity champion behavior'—behavior that is consistent, vocal, and impact driven. We want our associates in the store to be courageous and challenge one another about the values of diversity and in dealing with tough situations. We want to teach them to be resilient, learn to take risks, and understand the power of being vulnerable regardless of title."

GOING PUBLIC

The D&I office launched its Facebook page, A&F United: WORKING TOGETHER AS ONE, on May 5, 2011, managed of course by one of the Millennial's on my team, Ericka Jones. A&F United's page described its overall commitment and strategy for diversity that I drafted with important input from the team:

OUR COMMITMENT:

We are committed to embracing the diversity of our associates and management throughout our organization. On the surface, our dedication to maintaining a diverse working and shopping environment can be easily seen by walking through one of our stores, domestically and internationally. More notably, Abercrombie & Fitch's commitment can be seen through our exceptional diversity programs, whether they are internal or external, and the results they yield. Diversity reflects the multidimensional insights we share collectively. Simply put, it is imperative to our growth that we staff our business with diverse talent and run our business with an inclusive mindset.

OUR STRATEGY:

Our strategy for creating a more diverse and inclusive culture is focused on the elements and drivers of organizational change, including: Leadership Commitment, Employee Engagement, Measurement & Accountability, Communication, Training & Education, and Policy Integration. Individually, each driver plays a key role in maintaining our focus on Diversity & Inclusion, and collectively they allow us to audit the standards and processes that fuel our drive to be best in class.

The page had more than ten million friends-of-fans by 2013, and the D&I team working in partnership with the stores diversity council was also urging its associates—a term used to describe managers and brand reps—to spread its #EraseExclusion message on Instagram. The page was the vehicle for the company's annual Facebook Challenge during D&I Awareness Week, where regions researched and nominated charities to receive support. "The biggest question we get from associates is, 'how can we get involved more with nonprofit organizations and give back to our communities,'" the Challenge guidelines explain. "We know that our associates love to inspire change and give back to their communities and things that matter most to them."

In 2011, I asked longtime managers, including some who had lived through the *Gonzalez* era, to reflect on the company's diversity and inclusion evolution. When a worker in West Chicago came out as gay, his family cut him off, but Abercrombie & Fitch arranged a job where he could afford the commute, and one manager wrote:

We found him a spot in the city to help support him and help him get to a spot where he felt more comfortable. I'm proud to be part of a company where he felt comfortable coming to us for support.

The pride came from quarters where the company's failure had triggered the suit—Asians, Hispanics, African Americans, and women; and where it had more recently hit glitches—Muslims, internationals.

A woman who had heard of Abercrombie & Fitch's discrimination troubles in the classes where she was earning a degree in social work was reluctant to go to work for the company when she was recruited. She mentioned her concerns to the African American

District Manager and the Regional Recruiter who interviewed her and took the chance. "The inspiration I feel now and how it applies to my everyday life is amazing," she wrote.

> *I am so happy and proud to have seen and been a part of watching this company grow, since I started as a manager in 2005. I have a more open mind because of the growth this company has enabled." Other managers told similar stories.*

Noi, District Manager of multiple locations:

> *I'm most proud of having an opportunity to move forward with A&F as an Asian American female. I noticed during store manager training eight years ago that I was the only Asian in the room. Looking around today in the auditorium when all the DMs are gathered together, I see the improvements, the changes that we've made—not because of the consent decree, but because we have been doing the right thing.*

Jessie, District Manager in Los Angeles:

> *Coming from a very diverse environment, I never thought of diversity being something that was an issue. But we took this message as an opportunity to make everyone aware that it's more than just having diverse stores, but it is also making it an inclusive environment. I have also had my stores extremely involved in multiple charity events. My stores have become more aware of making their stores inclusive and more involved in their communities.*

Patty, District Manager in Atlanta:

> *I'm proud that I have gotten to work for a company that promotes based on results. I have never felt as though I've been promoted based on being a minority, or held back due to my ethnicity.*

Zinat, District Manager in Fort Worth:

> *I am proud of being a part of a company that did not discrim-*
> *inate against me for being a Muslim American female post*
> *9/11, even though I was the only diverse manager in my area at*
> *the time. It's also very exciting for me to be a part of increasing*
> *diversity within my own stores and for them to nominate me*
> *to be a diversity champion.*

Morgan, District Manager in Oberhausen, Germany:

> *I'm proud of the fact that with diversity and inclusion training,*
> *I have been more able to be a compassionate, caring manager;*
> *being able to bring diversity and inclusion international with*
> *all its different facets.*

Nick, District Manager in Houston:

> *Working for this company as a part-timer and a manager*
> *since 2000, I've been able to see the company grow so much in*
> *regards to diversity and inclusion. The way we are viewed from*
> *people outside the company now has changed so drastically*
> *as a result of the sponsorships, scholarships, and initiatives. It*
> *definitely makes me proud to tell people the company I work*
> *for.*

It was not by coincidence that the college students who pressed *Gonzalez* were the first wave of a new generation—the Millennials—that came of age at the turn of the twenty-first century and the confluence of historical, political, and demographic trends that signaled a decisive break with the past, including Abercrombie & Fitch's past. The generation that will see the United States become a majority-minority country inherited a world with accelerating connective technology and without the Cold War of their parents and grandparents. Forty percent of them have a close friend or family member of another race or ethnicity, compared to 3 percent of the older generations. They are heirs to the Civil Rights Movement they had not known, and, in general, they take the equality of other humans as a given, not a goal.

As a group, they are tolerant of almost anything except intolerance. Brandy Hawk had to hear her grandfather's Jim Crow experience before she recognized the injustice she had suffered, and the call to challenge it for the sake of others. Eduardo Gonzalez recoiled at exclusion in the avant-garde Bay Area. I recognized that the *Gonzalez* lawsuit came mercifully at the leading edge of such a generation, that the company could reposition itself to welcome the succeeding waves that would grow larger and ever more conscious of a company's social enlightenment, or lack of it.

In the process, the very notion of diversity was evolving. No one contemplated the case of a person with a prosthetic left arm, a Muslim woman in hijab, or a college student shopping for plus-sized clothing. Facebook started virtually the same time as Abercrombie's diversity strategy was being crafted, and Twitter was another two years off. A drive for social equality and human solidarity comes with no finish line to cross—even the election of an African American president could not end the call for continued effort in the generations-old Civil Rights Movement. Maybe we will have more luck at closing the wage gap between men and women when a woman is elected president.

The temptation of prejudice and "otherizing" lurks beneath the surface, ready to break out in an ill-advised and poorly thought out Instagram or Tweet, as I know, and the business consequences of such missteps can prove disastrous in the modern viral world. The price of equality is eternal vigilance. The bottom line is more and more dependent on the triple bottom line—people and planets as well as profits. The commitment to acceptance, respect, and inclusion of people, who are different, in whatever way, is vital in a diverse world, a world that every day looks more and more like the workforce of Abercrombie & Fitch's in-store population.

The evidence is clear that the emerging generation, the iGens (Generation Z), will sustain and expand the person-centered advances of the Millennials. Almost two years to the day of launching the diversity office's Facebook page, the commitment to inclusion and the diversity strategy was tested when, in May 2013, I saw the passion of Eduardo Gonzalez, alive in seventeen-year-old Cali Linstrom, a first-wave iGen from Chicago, spark a national discussion about corporate responsibility, body type, and bullying. The sequence of events opened the door for my team to be innovative once again, reiterating my mantra that inclusion trumps exclusion by creating an international anti-bullying program and call to action, "Are You An Ally?"

Now in its third year, the program appears to be structured and administered the way it was originally designed. As evidence of that, it remains anchored to the partnerships my team and I secured in its inaugural year: No Bully, a national not-for-profit based in San Francisco and The National Society of High School Scholars Foundation based in Atlanta. Moreover, the campaign kick-off in 2015 featuring the star power of pop rock band, Echosmith, whose song "Cool Kids" resonated with young people, was an effort to reach the genuine and heartfelt response that was visible during the 2013 launch, when the campaign was kicked off on New York's Lower West Side by Nina Davuluri, Miss America 2014. As the first Indian-American winner, she represented to the world that the girl next door is evolving as the diversity in America changes. She wrote, "people will internalize different messages than the ones I swallowed, and grow up believing that there are many different ways to be beautiful." A&F boasts that the program remains focused on leveraging student empathy to stop bullying and cyberbullying. They tout that "more than 20,000 U.S. schools have been supported and over $400,000 has reached nearly 1 million middle and high school students."

In 2013, the "Are You An Ally?" anti-bullying campaign, under the watchful eyes of Toya Spencer, my senior manager & lead trainer, and Shawn Knapp, my diversity analyst, toured twenty high schools across the United States with Linstrom urging students to adopt a broader understanding of how to relate to others. The program, which adopted materials developed by the Office of Diversity & Inclusion, was also featured in an anti-bullying curriculum simultaneously introduced in Seoul, South Korea, where the issue of bullying, according to experts, arises from the hyper-competitive nature of South Korean society.

"Cali has the idea of what she wants to do," I explained to *Racing Toward Diversity* magazine. "My team of trainers can think about how you have a conversation that's holistic. Companies aren't tying the conversations together, which we've been doing. It's going very well. At the end of the day, what's happening is these young people are getting a different definition of what they think inclusion means. It's linking the languages of inclusion rather than creating exclusion at the bus stop, in the lunchroom, in the band room.

"Cali has been bullied. She's been a bully. She's failed attempts at suicide. She's telling the story from both ends. Instantly, they see her as themselves and they don't challenge it. Every kid walks out of there feeling like they have a story to tell. It's one hundred to three hundred kids in a room. That small group of people, city by city, are starting to become something that kids around them can learn from."

"I was impressed with how receptive they were to our concerns, and how willing they were to make a commitment to take action against bullying and discrimination and support diversity and inclusion," Linstrom told *The Daily Beast*. The peer presentations moved high school freshmen to weep, share deeply personal stories, or break into song during the fifty-minute sessions with freshmen.

In addition to bullying based on race, gender, sexual orientation, and other familiar diversity issues, students are bullied because of their status as underclassmen, their neighborhoods, their hobbies, or their choice of extracurricular activities. Hazing, a form of bullying for people who wish to join an in-group, has led to highly publicized tragedies including the death of a band member at Florida A&M University in 2011. All of those things may be central to why a kid might be treated differently. The inclusive mindset has to transcend all that. "We're not perfect, but with the A&F D&I stuff, we pushed the envelope," I said. "We're not just trying to do the work inside and check a box. I'm trying to make sure a generation of people understands who we are, gets that we're doing things that are innovative and different, fresh and new. You've got to do a hard-hitting program that takes you from the inside to the outside."

Other things were involved in the campaign, but the real essence was the message of inclusion and exclusion, getting young people to think about diversity and inclusion in a way they hadn't thought about it. "Kids are now applying new and different dimensions of inclusion and exclusion to definitions of bullying—subtle nuances, treating people like you would want to be treated," I explained. "We're pushing kids to figure that out. We're trying to make this message a global message. Out of an unfortunate episode, we can come out of here with authenticity shaping the way you talk about it, a way that young people are made to be whole again."

My work at Abercrombie & Fitch was a long-term change management initiative, built with many layers and safeguards— safeguards that should be considered by anyone charged with implementing a diversity strategy. With them, you can mitigate the unforeseen events that hide in the weeds and threaten the authenticity of your diversity strategy's high aims. For the disciplined and thoughtful diversity executive or even the Chief HR Officer, culture transformation and inclusion initiatives are the keys to a successful diverse workplace.

As Daphne Howland wrote in RetailDIVE (July 10, 2014):

Corley is widely credited for changing the outward diversity of the clothing retailer, as well as its fundamental culture around inclusion and tolerance. Who knows whether Abercrombie & Fitch bargained for the corporate culture changes that Todd Corley ultimately brought, but under his direction the company has indeed changed immensely.

Chapter 9

A NEW PATH

That work, and that stage of my life, came to a conclusion on July 9, 2014, when Abercrombie & Fitch and I issued this press release:

ABERCROMBIE & FITCH ANNOUNCES NEW LEADERSHIP FOR ITS DIVERSITY & INCLUSION PROGRAMS

New Albany, OH, July 9, 2014: Abercrombie & Fitch (NYSE: ANF) announced that the Company has reorganized its Diversity & Inclusion structure. Todd Corley, who has led the Diversity & Inclusion efforts for the Company since 2004, is transitioning from the organization to launch the TAPO Institute, which will focus on inclusive leadership based on principles of transparency, authenticity, persistence, and optimism.

As part of its continuing commitment to diversity and inclusion, Abercrombie & Fitch will assign oversight of its Diversity & Inclusion efforts to Amy Zehrer, Executive Vice President of Stores. She will assume responsibility for all Home Office efforts and the Company's approximately 100,000 global store associates. Ms. Zehrer will continue to report to Mike Jeffries, Chief Executive Officer of the Company.

"As Chief Diversity Officer, Todd Corley created and implemented a transformational framework for our D&I efforts and we are thankful for everything he has contributed over his ten years with A&F," said Amy Zehrer. "We will further enhance the great work that has already been completed under Todd's leadership, such as our stores going from less than ten percent non-white associates to over 50% today. I look forward to the next stage of our efforts, and am energized to help further this initiative within our Home Office and our 1,000 stores around the world."

Notable recognition and achievements for the Company's diversity and inclusion efforts include:

- Being named a Best Place to work for the LGBT Community from 2007-2014; Receiving a perfect score from the Human Rights Campaign's Corporate Equality Index for eight consecutive years;

- Achieving significant gender diversity among its senior ranks, with over 40% of the Company's vice presidents, and 75% of executive vice presidents being female. In addition, one-third of directors on the Company's newly-constituted Board of Directors are female;

- Applying our framework on inclusion to anti-bullying efforts and making significant financial contributions to initiatives like the 2013 Anti-Bullying campaign, "Are You an Ally?";

- Establishing the A&F Global Diversity and Leadership scholarship program with the National Society of High School Scholars (NSHSS); and

- Establishing a Diversity & Inclusion training program with required participation for all Home Office, Distribution Center and Store Management associates.

"*I am proud of the accomplishments we have made together as an organization,*" *said Todd Corley. "The efforts began around race and ethnicity but evolved to include diversity in the way people think, cultural differences, and creating an inclusive place to work.*"

Mike Jeffries, CEO of Abercrombie & Fitch, said, "We are very grateful for the time Todd spent with A&F and all that he has helped achieve. We have accomplished so much, and I am confident that we will continue to maintain our high standards with diversity and inclusion, a cause to which the Company is strongly committed."

About Abercrombie & Fitch

Abercrombie & Fitch Co. is a leading global specialty retailer of high-quality, casual apparel for Men, Women and kids with an active, youthful lifestyle under its Abercrombie & Fitch, abercrombie, Hollister Co. and Gilly Hicks brands. At the end of the first quarter, the Company operated 842 stores in the United States and 157 stores across Canada, Europe, Asia and Australia. The Company also operates e-commerce websites at www.abercrombie.com, www.abercrombiekids.com, www.hollisterco.com and www.gillyhicks.com.

About The TAPO Institute

The TAPO Institute, a think tank and strategic advisor advocating inclusive leadership, draws its inspiration from today's generation being transparent, authentic, persistent and optimistic about inclusion. Visit tapoinstitute.org to learn more.

Media Contact: Public Relations
Abercrombie & Fitch
(614) 283-6192
Public_Relations@abercrombie.com

Driving along the curvy Fitch Path with the old office in my rearview mirror, I was excited about what would come next—a legacy for the hundreds of thousands of young people who had been my collaborators in work, laughter, debate, inspiration, and transformation. As a self-described "habitual listener," I soaked up every conversation I had over the years, whether it was my annual one-on-one meetings with the store organization's top brass—the Regional Managers and Store Directors—or those who were grinding it out every day across college campuses and minority career fairs, to identify new talent—the Store Recruiters. I also took great pride in teaching them to become more transparent and authentic. With a high degree of confidence, I think they would say that the relationship was beneficial to them in the end, as well.

Todd, it was just a few days ago I was talking to Nichole about you. I was wondering how you were doing and if A&F really appreciated or understood how your leadership has impacted those you've touched. I don't know that I can thank you enough for how you changed me as a leader. I realized my passion and success as a leader has come from engaging and inspiring those around me. You taught me that excuses and being "real and honest" are essentially the same, except for one fundamental difference…excuses lack accountability and lay blame, where being "real and honest" allows empowerment and accountability. To me that is where amazing starts to happen.

—Seth, former-Regional Manager, A&F, U.S. Southeast

Todd, similarly, you made a huge impression on me and the way I saw myself in a leadership role. You helped me challenge myself to be critical of how I could always do better and be better; and you did so in a unique way that was motivating and inspirational. You are absolutely missed at A&F by so many of us, and I wish you continued success with your next adventure ahead. You have been a champion to so many of us, and have helped inspire us to follow in your footsteps.

—Korrin, former-Regional Manager, A&F, Canada

Todd, I wanted to say thank you for everything you have done for me professionally but more importantly personally. Since meeting you, my eyes have been opened in more ways than I can explain. Growing up with A&F in a sense, I didn't realize how blinded I truly was, so thank you. I hope that we don't become strangers, and I wish you the absolute best in whatever your next journey is. I will cheer on your Hoyas as long as they aren't playing my alma mater in the tourney. Take care.

—Anonymous, Director at World Headquarters, Stores, — A&F and Hollister

I had chosen the name of the new organization, TAPO, and defined the acronym that lists its lofty goals: **T**ransparency, **A**uthenticity, **P**ersistence, and **O**ptimism. My experience convinced me that we can attain those aims through commitment and engagement. They are the keys to modern cultural transformation efforts.

Fifteen months after I left, I noticed that Abercrombie & Fitch's "newly" revised hiring policy, published on April 24, 2015, reads: "We hire nice, smart, and OPTIMISTIC people." However that language came to be included, optimism was certainly a key driver in the diversity success I oversaw and fought to maintain, and it is essential for creating any organization-wide inclusion effort, regardless of where you are on the implementation curve. Optimism is also a key piece to the guiding principles of inclusive leadership. My own optimism helped me and my team push through internal headwinds, rally the troops around the common goal of valuing and leveraging differences, and stay excited about the unique opportunity to partner with so many other young people on an incredible journey of self-reflection, vulnerability, and knowledge sharing.

Moreover, A&F's new policy language echoes the framework of the "inclusion wheel" we created several years earlier, where at least twenty-five characteristics of personal differences were regularly used as the icebreaker for onboarding new talent—translated in the local languages of global cities where we had stores, including Paris, Oberhausen, and Shanghai—to acknowledge how elaborately and broadly Millennials and iGens defined themselves and now demand to be understood.

New waves of Millennials continue to press for diversity and inclusion, even today in 2015. The case involving Samantha Elauf, now in her twenties, is an example of that – her case on religious accommodations (*EEOC v. Abercrombie & Fitch*) was decided in her favor by the Supreme Court in an 8–1 decision.

GUIDING PRINCIPLES FOR MANAGING THE GENERATIONAL SHIFT

In my roles as former Chief Diversity Officer at Abercrombie & Fitch and current Board Chair of the National Society of High School Scholars Foundation, my job has always involved engaging the younger generations on issues of civic participation, inclusion, and social responsibility. I am constantly trying to understand what they want and what is relevant to them. Today's young people have taught me a new set of goals, an orientation to the elements of a different kind of self-understanding and social connection that reflects the new world they are creating. I organized the large categories in my mind as TAPO—Transparency, Authenticity, Persistence, and Optimism. These qualities have become central for me, not only as what I expect from others but also what I expect from myself.

Transparency. Millennials and iGens want to see what's really going on—not just the surface outcome, but the depth of intention, of context, of assumptions, premises, and logical steps. Their whole lives have been in the Information Age, and they have a reflexive suspicion when they believe information is being withheld. They do not accept the superior-knows-best attitude prevalent in the past, they are not willing to do their jobs without thinking, and they believe their perspectives should be respected. They are willing to be transparent to others—they have a refreshing, matter-of-fact frankness about their own foibles and shortcomings as well as their strengths and successes—and they expect the same.

They ask "Why?" far more than previous generations, and they demand an answer. When they believe they've heard an honest reply, they are far more willing to understand the policy and follow the direction. Even if the initial reaction is negative, they are willing to change their minds based on evidence. This became vivid to me during an October 2014 trip to Marrakesh, where I attended the *Atlantic Dialogues*. The German Marshall Fund (GMF) Emerging Leaders challenged a room filled with world leaders who were dripping with degrees and accolades. These young people insisted that transforming the transatlantic dialogue into real change requires starting the conversation with the life of people at the local level, with a governance framework anchored in resilience and not clouded by hidden agendas that hinder progress.

Authenticity. Through the transparent honesty, Millennials and iGens expect to see authentic thoughts, actions, and people. If transparency exposes hypocrisy, they will balk. They would rather engage a person who honestly disagrees than one who dishonestly agrees. Authenticity involves consistency, reliability, and sustainability. What you see is what you get—and what you get must be as honest, dependable, supportive, dedicated, and as available tomorrow as it is today. Transparency makes authenticity far more important than it was when people accepted conclusions at face value and questions about leaders' motives, calculations, and rewards were considered out of bounds.

The January–February 2015 issue of the *Harvard Business Review* considers this issue in its cover story: "The Problem with Authenticity." In short, if we concede that authenticity is a key ingredient for successful leadership, then we must make room for it and not waver. The risks from failure to do this have implications across the globe in every sector—public and private. For instance, a lack of authentic leadership hobbles efforts to create alignment between policies and programs that may mitigate poverty, close the education gap, and rebuild dilapidated neighborhoods.

Persistence. Persistence for Millennials and iGens has less to do with sticking to a particular job, the "work ethic" focus for earlier generations, and more to do with improving oneself—professional skills, personal interactions, and willingness to think out of the box and step out of the comfort zone. Older people, accustomed to focusing only on the task, sometimes scorn this broader view, but it likely makes the younger people more productive, not less. Their overarching dynamic, evolving world view leaves no room for ultimate finish lines or static repetition. Their continuous improvement can apply to job processes, but above all it is personal and extends beyond the workplace. They are willing to do whatever it takes, in their jobs as in their relationships—and they understand that it takes more than technical skills or punch-clock hours.

Optimism. The focus on openness, authenticity, and improvement provides Millennials with a fundamental optimism. They view the world in personal terms, not primarily through the economic lens like many of their parents and grandparents. Technology has created connected communities and borderless discussion groups, where ideas and solutions are freely exchanged.

Even in the midst of a financial collapse and the heavy debt that many carry, they are able to see the world changing for the better. They are a major driver of that change, especially when it comes to recognizing the rights and dignity of others. They live in a world of possibility, determined that there would be no oppressors and no oppressed. They believe they have the tools as well as the spirit to effect change, and they are confident that the arc of history bends toward justice.

To paint a picture of what our new world would look like, if the aforementioned categories were embraced and actually ushered in a new normal, let me share with you an excerpt that I was drawn to from this year's Y20 Summit held in Istanbul, Turkey, on August 19, 2015. Started in 2010 as an initiative of voluntary non-governmental non-profit youth organizations and individuals, the Y20 Summit is constituted to enable Millennials and iGens from around the world to raise issues for the G20 Summit leaders to consider and debate.

My connection to the Y20 Summit is a Millennial named Carlos, who was one of five U.S. delegates among 110 from around the world gathering to consider major topics such as education, technology, and youth unemployment. He and I first met at an event for the National Society of High School Scholars, several years earlier. As a group, Carlos and his peers submitted the following recommendations to the G20 cabinet:

We (Y20) strongly urge G20 countries to use education as a tool for social cohesion, tolerance and celebration of diversity by:

a. promoting sensitivity towards the struggles of the disenfranchised and respect for diversity, through the enhancement of civic and national peace education curricula, as defined by the United Nations (UN) that aims to eliminate bullying and prevent youth radicalization, as well as to raise a society that promotes a culture of peace;

b. addressing social inequalities by guaranteeing continuous access, outside of teaching hours, to educational and communal spaces, as well as sufficient access to free language courses for children with migratory and minority backgrounds.

We (Y20) urge G20 countries to improve Early Childhood Development by creating interactive parent-focused projects, programs and workshops as well as strengthening intensive forms of help for children with special needs.

We (Y20) recommend G20 countries to reduce the skills mismatch between the education system and the labor market by:

a. increasing students' access to information on labor market conditions, for example by publishing higher education rankings that prioritize graduate employment rates, teaching quality, and promoting the use of guidance counsellors;

b. improving communication between employers and education providers to ensure that education includes a focus on teaching relevant skills, particularly in STEAM subjects and coding courses, by encouraging education providers to take steps to limit graduate unemployment;

c. promoting the role of internships and work experience as an element of tertiary education and ensuring that students have access to fair remuneration or support in accordance with national labor rights.

We (Y20) urge G20 countries to recognize that demographic change requires a greater availability of learning opportunities in professional life, and therefore encourage the public, private, and non-profit sectors to design new and expand existing youth initiatives, traineeships, and vocational trainings to:

a. strengthen intergenerational solidarity and skills transfers;

b. better align the skills and needs of new and aging workers to the changing needs of the marketplace through the expansion of lifelong learning opportunities.

We (Y20) urge G20 countries to introduce sustainable economic education from the secondary level, including:

a. education which teaches cost-benefit analysis and personal finance to develop decision making skills in the economic field;

b. teaching general economics, to increase conscious partic-

ipation in the economic and political debate and to raise awareness about sustainable development issues.

We (Y20) urge G20 countries [to] promote student international mobility and expand opportunities to increase students' chance in seeking quality education and experience sharing by simplifying the visa granting procedure for students and young scientists, including the reduction of costs and simplification of the visa delivery system.

Due to the gap in the quality of education between rural, underdeveloped and urban areas, we (Y20) urge G20 countries to guarantee basic educational infrastructure and services, including internet access, in conjunction with the provision of support systems to encourage education attendance and online cross-degrees.

To read the entire Y20 Summit Communiqué, visit the Y20 Summit website. However, whether you visit the site or not, consider this – if even some of what the group urged is accomplished over time, how better off would we all be in the end?

STRATEGIES FOR MANAGING THE GENERATIONAL SHIFT

Many organizations are not prepared or are ill equipped to handle the shift in values that young workers are bringing. The future has arrived, and if you're not careful, your organization will become a failed relic. Here are a few tips on what you should be aware of and how you should assess those situations:

- **Identify headwinds and crosswinds**.

  The prevailing winds of business can make a huge difference in the amount of effort a company has to exert to be successful. These winds come as either "headwinds" (top-down resistance) or "crosswinds" (peer-to-peer resistance). In the latter case, peers may actively or passively stifle progressive steps for creating meaningful (but perhaps not popular) changes by either blocking or tackling while you are implementing new policies or programs. In any case, you should identify other influential leaders in the organization that can reinforce your agenda for change. Don't underestimate *anyone* in the organization; often, the voices you need to make change are not on the leadership team or inner circle. People who have an outside view of the terrain might better help you cross rocky stretches. Moreover, don't be shy about recruiting people who have the influence you need and then eventually "planting" them strategically in the organization as your advocates. If they're in place and you've vetted them, you'll know that they are ready to remove the detractions and distractions on a moment's notice.

- **Ask for forgiveness rather than permission.**

  Whether your role in culture change is large or small, the only thing that matters is your legacy. Building that legacy is more enjoyable when you take calculated risks, put it all on the line, and push the envelope. If you tend to doubt yourself and your goals, you're likely looking for "red light, green light" commands. Embrace ambiguity and believe that your brainstorm idea can lead to a breakthrough moment. If you ask permission, you have to live with a "no" answer; if you act and fall short, you can ask forgiveness. Over my life, I've always operated on the principle that it's better to ask for forgiveness than ask for permission. Today's generations are unlike any we have ever seen. They expect us to be quick, nimble, and vulnerable when we engage them, and to provide them with purposeful challenges. This is not a call to be reckless, but it is a warning to be less rigid and predictable.

- **Find an unlikely friend.**

   Your appreciation and embrace of the generational shift in values will depend on how well you know someone (across each of the five generational groups in the workplace) and see their perspective. It is incredibly helpful and liberating, most days, to have that "unlikely friend" stretch your comfort zone. In such a relationship, you may need to set ground rules for civility, because you may not agree on points that are important to you and vice versa. What will become apparent over time is that your willingness to tussle and freely exchange ideas across the aisle opens you up to a world of new ideas and skills.

- **Let it hang in the balance.**

   Physical distance is much less significant to the new workforce and even less so for Generation Z, as they have the ability to interact with people in places that they may have never visited or even find on a map. Implicit in that reality is that we do not need to hover over the least experienced person on the team—fresh out of college or even the summer intern—because he or she is inevitably going to figure out how to manage through the task at hand. Simply put, if people with less experience don't know the answer, someone in their circle of friends—or a friend of a friend—does know the right answer. The odds are always on their side. Trust them.

- **Stay unzipped and unbuttoned.**

   Presenting a false sense of who you are to a generation that knows about you before you open your mouth—hint, hint, a Google search—is a complete turnoff. I am not suggesting that you completely strip down to the bare bones, but I am saying that vulnerability is much sexier these days than critics give it credit. Find a personal story that you are comfortable sharing and learn how to tell the story in a number of different settings—for example, the holiday party, the company retreat, or the lunch table—so that when you tell it, people can connect it to you and hear it in its authentic voice. A little reveal shows that you're confident in yourself and that you want people around you to be who they really are.

- **Manage the moment's in-between.**

  Anticipating when a Millennial or iGen is ready for the next challenge is key to engagement. Their ability to multitask and push through assignments with an eye on the next one often causes frustration with managers, who are not thinking about what happens in-between one project and the next. Consider giving employees the option to identify a social cause they would like to take part in, as well as offer them extra time to volunteer or run their own donation campaigns. Knowing how socially conscious these generations are and the rise of social activism, this type of opportunity could be the difference between their believing that your organization is truly committed to causes with a "purpose" versus being a brand only focused on "profit."

- **Get rid of the kiddie table.**

  It is imperative to offer employees the appropriate motivation, time, and tools to understand how their work and your organization are both contributing to the big picture. You can try implementing an 80-20 rule like Google, offering your employees time away from the office to be inspired. Those moments allow them to see how their sweat equity can turn one simple idea into a radical transformation. Jen, a manager in her thirties, shared with me as I was writing this book that all she ever wanted from the employer she just left was to be trusted. Her words exactly were, "I did not realize how much I actually knew until I started interviewing and having conversations with hiring managers and vice presidents at competitor brands. It built my confidence significantly, which is good momentum to have when I start my new job."

These tips are not only rooted in years of consulting experience, working on the inside and pushing for reform. A recent report issued by The Leadership Center for Inclusion at Deloitte University (Deloitte Consulting) confirms what I know to be true: Millennials are intolerant of workplaces that don't allow them to be themselves. "The Radical Transformation of Diversity and Inclusion: The Millennial Influence," released in 2015, concludes that Millennials view inclusion as having a "culture of connectedness that facilitates teaming, collaboration and professional growth." In their mind, leadership must be "supportive of individual perspectives, while being transparent, communicative and engaging."

Stephanie Turner, PhD, who is one of the authors of the study, and I participated in a conference together in Washington, D.C. on August 13, 2015. We discussed with an esteemed panel the impact these changes would have on the workplace. Among her many great insights, what stuck out for me was the notion that Millennials report higher levels of engagement when operating in an inclusive culture. In fact, the Deloitte research study shows that 83 percent of Millennials are actively engaged when they believe the organization fosters an inclusive culture. Comparatively, 60 percent of Millennials are actively engaged when they believe the organization does not have an inclusive culture. The simple translation: if you don't engage them, someone else will (about every two years or so, when they move from one employer to another), and the money you've spent recruiting and developing them will adversely impact your bottom line.

This book serves as a cautionary tale for every organization that has some connection to recruiting, retaining or resonating with todays "new workforce". Fortunately, it is completely within reach for the current majority of Baby Boomer and Gen X managers to challenge their traditional approaches to leadership, embrace behavioral patterns that promote and advocate for non-judgmental inquiry, and break down the barriers of resistance so they can become inclusive-minded and transformational leaders.

SOURCES

"2013 Demographics: Profile of the Military Community," *Military Onesource*. Office of the Deputy Assistant Secretary of Defense, 2013. Web. 6 October 2015.

"Age Distribution by Religious Group (2014)." *Pew Research Center*. Pew Research Center, 2014. 8 October 2015.

"Are Young People Watching Less TV? (Updated – Q2 2015 Data)." *MarketingCharts*. Watershed Publishing, 29 September 2015. Web. 7 October 2015.

Bloom, Nicholas, James Liang, John Roberts, and Zhichun Jenny Ying. "Does Working from Home Work? Evidence from a Chinese Experiment." *The Quarterly Journal of Economics* (2015) 165-218. Web. 7 October 2015.

"Chapter One: A Portrait of Smartphone Ownership." *U.S. Smartphone Use in 2015*. Pew Research Center, 1 April 2015. Web. 7 October 2015.

Cohn, D'Vera. "Falloff in births slows shift to a majority-minority youth population." *Fact Tank: News in the Numbers*. Pew Research Center, 26 June 2014. Web. 7 October 2015.

Dunsmuir, Lindsay and Maurice Tamman. "Many Americans have no friends of another race: poll." *Reuters*. Thomson Reuters, 8 August 2013. Web. 7 October 2015.

"Election Center 2008 Exit Polls." *Election Center 2008*. Cable News Network LP, 2004. Web. 6 October 2015.

Fry, Richard. "A Rising Share of young Adults Live in Their Parent's Home." *Pew Research Center*. Pew Research Center, 1 August 2013. Web. 7 October 2015.

---. "Millennials Surpass Gen Xers as the Largest Generation in U.S. Labor Force." *Pew Research Center*. Pew Research Center, 11 May 2015. Web. 6 October 2015.

Gottlieb, Sherry. *Hell No, We Won't Go*. New York: Viking Adult, 1991. Print.

Hammond, Teena. "Research: 74 percent using or adopting BYOD." *ZDNet*. CBS Interactive, 5 January 2015. Web. 7 October 2015.

"Household Debt and Credit Report." *The Center for Microeconomic Data*. Federal Reserve Bank of New York, 2015. Web. 7 October 2015.

Internet Live Stats. International Telecommunication Union and United Nations Population Division and Internet & Mobile Association of India and World Bank, 1 July 2014. Web. 7 October 2015.

Knowle, Valerie. *Forging Our Legacy: Canadian Citizenship and Immigration*, 1990-1977. Ottawa: Citizenship and Immigration Canada, 2000. Print.

Maron, Dina. "Early Puberty: Causes and Effects." *Scientific America* 312.5 (2015). Web. 7 October 2015.

"Mobile Technology Fact Sheet." *Pew Research Center*. Pew Research Center, October 2014. Web. 7 October 2015.

Moore, Gordon. "Cramming More Components into Integrated Circuits." *Electronics* 38.8 (1965): 114-117. Web. 7 October 2015.

"Network TV: Evening News Overall Viewership Since 1980." *News Media Indicators Database*. Pew Research Center, November 2014. Web. 7 October 2015.

Nielsen, Jakob. "Nielsen's Law of Internet Bandwidth." *Nielsen Norman Group*. Nielsen Norman Group, 5 April 1998. Web. 7 October 2015.

"Opinion on Legalizing Marijuana: 1969-2015." *Pew Research Center*. Pew Research Center, 14 April 2015. Web. 7 October 2015.

Ou, Yanwen, Emma Rose McGlone, Christian Fielder Camm, and Omar A. Khan. "Does playing video games improve laparoscopic skills?" *International Journal of Surgery* 11.5 (2013) 365-369. Web. 7 October 2015.

Rosser Jr., James C., Paul J. Lynch, Laurie Cuddihy, Douglas A. Gentile, Jonathan Klonsky, and Ronald Merrell. "The Impact of Video Games on Training Surgeons in the 21st Century." *Arch Surgery* 142.2 (2007) 181-186. Web. 7 October 2015.

Snyder, Howard N.. "Arrest in the United States, 1990-2010." *U.S. Department of Justice Statistics* (2012). Web. 7 October 2015.

"Stop-and-Frisk Data." *New York Civil Liberties Union*. New York Civil Liberties Union, 2015. Web. 7 October 2015.

"Stream Engines: Subscription Video Services Give Options to Consumers Looking to Spend on Content." *Nielsen*. The Nielsen Company, 11 march 2015. Web. 7 October 2015.

"Thanks to Strong Sales, Vinyl Albums are off and Spinning." *Nielsen*. The Nielsen Co, 16 April 2015. Web. 7 October 2015.

"The Student Loan Landscape." *Liberty Street Economics*. Federal Reserve Bank of New York, 18 February 2014. Web. 7 October 2015.

Thurman, Susan. "NSHSS Scholar 2015 Millennial Career Survey Results." *National Society of High School Scholars*. National Society of High School Scholars, 2015. Web. 6 October 2015.

Touryalai, Halah. "Student Loan Problems: One Third of Millennials Regret Going to College." *Forbes*. Forbes, 22 May 2013. Web. 7 October 2015.

"Unemployment Rate." *Bureau of Labor Statistics*. United States Department of Labor, 2015. Web. 6 October 2015.

"U.S. President / National / Exit Poll." *Election 2004*. Cable News Network LP, 2004. Web. 6 October 2015.

Wang, Wendy. "The Rise of Intermarriage." *Pew Research Center*.

Pew Research Center, 16 February 2012. Web. 7 October 2015.

---. "Interracial Marriage: Who is 'marrying out'?" *Pew Research Center*. Pew Research Center, 12 June 2015. Web. 7 October 2015.

ACKNOWLEDGEMENTS

Thanks, to the **hundreds of thousands of associates** that supported my vision for inclusion, across the 20+ countries, where Abercrombie & Fitch had a presence. Your efforts taught me and thousands more, what inclusive behavior should look like.

A special thanks to the many external partners and collaborators, who encouraged me to push through the headwinds and crosswinds. Absent your words of encouragement, it would have made the journey less interesting.

For those not listed below, my sincerest apologizes for missing your name – you are indeed no less important.

- Toya Spencer
- Shawn Knapp
- Ericka Jones
- Elisia Dickison
- Sara Mellon
- Stephen Little
- Cincy Carraro
- Al Lundy
- Joe Sanchez
- Jen (Rupert) Sanchez
- Chad Moorefield
- Chris Parmentar
- Jessica Passaslacqua
- Josh Burris
- Frank Ha
- Nicole Falcone
- Patricia van Kleef
- Shane Berry
- Stacia Jones
- Nick Jozwiak
- Ramzi Bivens
- Kristen Guest
- Krista Gaskil
- Andrea Watson
- Lyndsey Schaap
- Shamika Marsh
- Amisha Rathod
- Julie Sims
- Kellee Farren
- Matt Kamigawachi
- Shanna Bush
- Ty Griffith
- Cynthia Fernandez
- Kai Roddeck

- Keethan Kitt
- Kevin Smith
- Kristin Horning
- Mandy Chrusz
- Megan Netschke
- Nik Porter
- Pam Tapia
- Regina Park
- Jamaul Joseph
- Sara Schwint
- Zinat Najafi
- Steve Delich
- Travis Clark
- Seana Meehan
- Adrianne Hardy
- Andrew Thompson
- Cassidy Hernandez
- Chris Clayton
- Jen Baptiste
- Jen Clarke
- Jill Gordon
- Justin Lewis
- Kris Akahosi
- Larisa Yarmchuck
- Michelle Stefano
- Nicole Slott
- Rachel Graffagnini
- Travis Johnson
- Trish Horrimoto
- Allison Demarch
- Amanda Varney
- Amber Rodriquez
- Ashley Page
- Bernice Wong
- Chris Samples
- Dave Toma
- Dinesh Penugonda
- Jennifer Butler
- Matteo Ward
- Raquel Mejia
- Samantha Dack
- Samantha Stovall
- James Igoea
- Tahmina Raquib
- Claudia Gozzi
- Will Herring
- Gus Perez
- Michelle Iaconis
- Lehua Fukumoto
- Stephanie Lau
- Nick Murdick
- Chris Lape
- Sarah Riviera
- Alex Benedetti
- Alexandria Letterman
- Amila Gacanica
- Alycia Taylor
- Chris Arbeene
- John Schaffner
- Nate Andres
- Andy Wourms
- James Roth
- Corey Routh
- Reggie Butler
- Gen Coleman
- Vincent Randolph Brown
- Fabian J. De Rozario
- Dena Shilling
- Anne Hackman
- Blake Hoyle

- Bonnie Costello
- Brett Gordon
- Dave Ogle
- David Newsom
- Dayna Perillo
- Jim Coughlin
- Justin Brannon
- Kathy Bachar
- Korrin Wallin
- Megan Watumull
- Meredith Maclean
- Michael Barrow
- Russ Mifsud
- Scott Lis
- Stephanie Burris
- Trae White
- Andy Wheeler
- Brendan Irvine
- Ernest Adams
- Leanne Boggs
- Kevin Force
- Erick Hoffman
- Dana Johnson
- Kerrie Depot
- Logan Ridgeway
- Jay Trainer
- Every DIVERSITY CHAMPION-recipient
- Every (DIVERSITY) Recruiter-hired
- Every RM, DM that believed in the work of "creating inclusion"

ABOUT THE AUTHOR:
TODD CORLEY

Todd Corley is the founder of The TAPO Institute, a blended think tank and advisory group focusing on the generationally-driven shift in beliefs and values that has redefined the meaning of "inclusive" leadership.

Prior to his role at Abercrombie & Fitch, Todd created the diversity strategy for Starwood Hotels & Resorts Worldwide as their diversity lead. He was also a senior consultant and the New York office team leader for Towers Perrin's global diversity and change management practice. During his tenure at Towers Perrin (now Towers Watson), his major client engagements were with The New York Stock Exchange, JPMorganChase and UBS PaineWebber. Specific to UBS, Todd was their in-house executive-on-loan working alongside the President. Other notable clients included: Toys R Us, American Express, Pepsi Co., Pfizer, and AstraZeneca.

Todd has received numerous awards and accolades that underscore his character and personal brand. Among the most notable, in 2013 he was presented with the inaugural "*Claes Nobel World Betterment Award*" by Mr. Claes Nobel, the senior-member of the esteemed family that established the Nobel Prize, for his commitment to global unity. He also serves as Board Chair for The National Society of High School Scholars Foundation, serving 1M+ Millennials and iGens across 160 countries. He is an active member of the Executive Leadership Council (ELC), the premier network of black executives. ELC members are black CEO's (current and former), corporate-board members, and senior executives at Fortune 500 companies.

In October 2014, he was invited to participate in the annual *Atlantic Dialogues* in Marrakesh, Morocco, discussing "Diversity as an Asset: Gender and Equity in the Atlantic Basin". Since its inception, The Atlantic Dialogues has emerged as the premier annual forum for globally focused decision-makers across the public- and private-sectors to discuss cross-regional issues and shared policy challenges shaping the future of the four continents around the Atlantic Basin.

Todd has an MBA from Georgetown University and is a graduate of the inaugural Brand & Reputation Management Program from Tuck Executive Education at Dartmouth. He resides in a suburb north of Columbus, Ohio, with his wife G.P. Fleming, M. D. and their two children, Olivia and Austin.

Made in the USA
Middletown, DE
15 March 2016